Girl, Get A Grip!

A Woman's Guide to Surviving Adversity

Francesca L. Stubbs

ISBN-13: 978-1499686234 (CreateSpace-Assigned)
ISBN-10: 1499686234

Cover Art by Purposed to Design Graphics
Printed in USA by CreateSpace
Published by SODAAN Publishing

Dedication

This book is dedicated to my children and their children's children and every generation thereafter. I leave the words on the following pages as a prophetic utterance for you and as a recorded word of healing, peace, wholeness of relationships, hope for a greater future, and liberty from every bondage. May these words speak to you personally. Every syllable, phrase and verse shall transcend time, eternity and generations; Even as the young king Josiah in Scripture finding that his name had been written in the Chronicles of the Kings (I Kings 13:2), three hundred years before his birth, set him on course to fulfilling his purpose of reviving and restoring the Glory of God to Israel- Even so, I decree every question you have be answered, that you receive Keys that set you free and give you authority to loose your seed and its generations from every yoke, allowing you to discover and accomplish the Will of God that has been ordained for you before the foundation of the world.

I loved you before you were ever born and I have prayed for you. For I know the day will come for you to read these words as you search for meaning and your purpose in this life, your history-both natural and spiritual shall come full circle. It is my prayer that you find part of it here. As you read, run with all your heart. Accomplish what I could not or did not. You are meant to be here. You belong here. It's your time. Complete your life's assignment and as I have left this decree for you, I admonish you to do the same for the generations after you that you will never see. Never forget that this work, and mantle is bigger than you, but God has graced you and these prophetic words will be for you, your weapon to war a good warfare. You SHALL accomplish ALL that God has designed for our generations.

Though I may have crossed the veil of eternity by the time this book reaches your hands, know this, I stand with the great cloud of witnesses in the next realm and we are cheering you on! Now grab the baton and RUN!!! WE are counting on you for our reward.

With love and prayers that cross the bands of eternity,

Your Matriacrch

(2 Kings 22; Eph. 3:3-6; Heb. 11:39; 12:1-2)

3

Table of Contents

Foreword

To the Wives who are in loveless marriages, the mothers who are mistreated and constantly disrespected by the fruit of your womb that you carried for 9 months and gave your all for, to the sisters who are always giving and never see reciprocity in the measure given, to the prayer warriors who can't seem to find a prayer partner to perservere with you, to the all around go to gal, who everyone else calls on and relies on but you can't seem to find anyone to call on and rely on, to all of the underdogs, the seemingly forgotten, to the cast aside who are hurting, GIRL, GET A GRIP!! You have gotten this far by God's grace and love. It has been hard. You don't even know how you got to where you are...GIRL, KEEP YOUR GRIP! Payday is coming! Your pain is not unnoticed. Your private tears are seen. Your bleeding heart is felt. God will not leave you comfortless. Know this day, you are on His mind and He wants you to know-Joy is coming! Love is Coming! Healing is coming! Respect and Honor are coming! Reciprocity for all you've sown is coming..in FULL MEASURE. You can't quit now. Help is on the way. So, GIRL, GET A GRIP!!!

I LOVE YOU MY SISTERS!!!

My Appreciation

Special Thanks to an awesome group of people who were very instrumental to the release and launch of this book. First, to my Spiritual Daughter and Editor, Danielle Smith. Words see inadequate to express my gratitude for your time and talent. I love you and appreciate you! To my launch team, (too many to name) than you so much for sowing into my life and ministry. Your invaluable feedback made a world of difference. Thank you x's 1000!!!

To my Spiritual Father Apostle Ricci Hausley for the balance you have bought to my life as a father, I am grateful. The long conversations (filled with life lessons), for your "CARE", and forever teaching your sons and daughters the importance of relationship, THANK YOU! You and Pastor Theresa are truly gems.

Finally, to my Spiritual Mother, Apostle Carolyn L. Hicks. There is so much that is owed to you in honor! You have poured out and it has been what I have learned from you in the past that has allowed me to become who I am today. You already know how much you mean to me. I love you and thank God for you and the impartation I have received from your life. I'm still watching and learning! I love you to LIFE!!

Introduction

Ladies and Gentlemen, it takes courage to deal with your pain, because it's sensitive. When you can begin to harness that courage to deal with the issues of life that hold you down, then you can begin to LIVE life the way God intended!

Let's covenant together to deal with it so we can be made whole and L I V E!!!

#Deal With It!!

Chapter One

Free To Be Me

There is so much fighting against our womanhood and our ability to be effective. Here, in the area where I live, there is a stronghold, which causes a fight for women to hold any type of leadership position in the church. I want to take the time to share some Scriptural points as well as life experiences which I believe will be invaluable as well as an encouragement to any other women who are facing the same struggles; whether it be in Corporate America or the Corporate Body of Christ, the struggle is indeed real it must be addressed if women will ever truly be "free" to be who they have been created to be.

We are going to look at John 8:31-47 in the English Standard Version . " So Jesus said to the Jews who had believed him, "If you abide in my word, you are truly my disciples, and you will know the truth, and the truth will set you free. They answered him, We are offspring of Abraham and have never been enslaved to anyone. How is it that you say, 'You will become free'? Jesus answered them, Truly, truly, I say to you, everyone who practices sin is a slave to sin. The slave does not remain in the house forever; the son remains forever. So if the Son sets you free, you will be free indeed. I know that you are offspring of Abraham; yet you seek to kill me because my word finds no place in you. I speak of what I have seen with my Father, and you do what you have heard from your father. They answered him, Abraham is our father." Jesus said to them, "If you were Abraham's children, you would be doing the works Abraham did, but now you seek to kill me, a man who has told you the truth that I heard from God. This is not what Abraham did. You are doing the works your father did." They said to him, "We were not born of sexual immorality. We have one Father— even God. Jesus said to them, "If God were your Father, you would love me, for I came from God and I am here. I came not of my own accord, but he sent me. 4Why do you not understand what I say? It is because you cannot bear to hear my word. You are of your father the devil, and your will is to do your father's desires. He was a murderer from the beginning, and does not stand in the truth, because there is no truth in him. When he lies, he speaks out of his own character, for he is a liar and the father of lies. 45 But because I tell the truth, you do not believe me. Which one of you convicts me of sin? If I tell the truth, why do you not believe me? 4Whoever is of God hears the words of God. The reason why you do not hear them is that you are not of God."

I was reading this and the Lord was really speaking me. I told the Lord that I wanted to be able to encourage the women of God, whether they carried a title of not. When we're thinking about the theme, "Free to Be Me", the only way that we are going to be able to be free is that we embrace the truth. We know that Jesus is talking about salvation here, so I am not going to exegete the text. We are just going to roll with some revelation here.

Here it is that Jesus is trying to help them to understand that the true liberty that they are going to be able to have is going to come when they understand that their identity is hid with Him. With us, if we are going to be able to be productive and be what God wants us to be, we have to be able to understand that even in the midst of carrying many things, we still have liberty. We have to deal with circumstances of life, stress from bills, trying to be a good wife, trying to be a good mom, trying to pastor the church, and all of these weights - however, we must understand that though we have weights, the weights don't have us. Sometimes our life will have a grip on us and that becomes a problem for us.

In looking at verse 31, we see that Jesus says to the Jews, *"If you abide in my word, you are truly my disciples."* I need you to understand that you have got to let this Word live in you. This is the only thing that is going to give you the strength to be able to fight against everything that is telling you that you are not who God says you are. It is important for us to really embrace our identity in Christ. We are so much more than we give ourselves credit for. We haven't even really been able to embrace everything God has for us. God wants us to be able to look into Him so that He can show us what it is that He has created us to do.

Jesus says to His disciples in verse 32: *"and you will know the truth, and the truth will set you free." The world has a saying, "This is your truth and this is my truth."* Truth cannot be changed. It's the truth in the morning and in the afternoon. Facts can change, and something can be "true" but not be truth. The truth of the matter is that we are born of God, and because we are born of God, that changes everything. You have to be able to really tell yourself what God's truth is because where we come from has tried to dictate to us who we are. We feel that because we are "so-and-so's daughter" and because of what our parents did growing up, we are prevented from being effective or even being happy for that matter. What we have to begin to do is to really look into ourselves. We then have to look into God's Word and allow the Word to live in us. You are going to have to eat this word like you eat food every day. You have to eat this word until everything about you changes and you understand that no matter the circumstance or situation you're facing, you're still free.

If I'm free to be me, who would I be? That's the question you have to ask yourself. Who are you going to be? You aren't going to be able to find your identity just in your job. What if you change jobs? You're not going to be able to find your identity because you're "so-and-so's wife". What if you unfortunately get divorced? That's a reality of life. We don't want you to get divorced, but what if you get divorced and you aren't Mrs. Jones anymore? What is your identity? Your identity is not in any of those things. If you are free to be who you are, whom do you choose to be? The thing about it is that you have to choose to be who God says you are. You can't let anybody else define you or confine you. People will try to bring definition to who you are and tell you who you are and then they will try to confine you by locking you in and saying, "You can only do this right here."

Let me give you a couple of definitions because I'm a teacher by nature. The word confine means: to restrict, to shut or keep in, to limit, to restrain or to put boundaries on. When I read these definitions I said to myself, "God, this is what has been happening to the women of God." We get saved, we get excited about Jesus, we want to do the will of God, and then we start going through trials. We start listening to people. We start dealing with all of our insecurities: not feeling like we're cute enough, thinking our butt is too big, not having a butt, etc. We have all of these things and we put restrictions on ourselves. We constrain ourselves and put boundaries on ourselves because what we're looking at in the mirror is telling us something else. The Word of God is the mirror you must look in to see who you really are. I don't care if you grew up in abuse. I don't care if you went through molestation when you were growing up. I don't care who left you, who walked away, who said you weren't worthy, who said you weren't too cute, who said you had a bad attitude, who said your breath stinks, who said your feet stinks - I don't care what they say. Your identity has nothing to do with that. I'm going to be honest. I've been through some things these past three years that have tested my identity. I have had to stand and talk to people who didn't believe that I am who God says I am. I began to look in the Scripture and I discovered that this was the same thing that Jesus went through. You're good as long as you're coming to church and doing everything that everyone wants you to do, but when God begins to reveal to you what He created you to do and be, people who really just want to keep you constrained and confined will not want you to do what God wants you to do. They are comfortable with us doing what fits into their boundaries and limitations. We are going to take all of those limitations off because we want to soar in the things of God. We want God to use us. We want God to have His way in our lives, and we want to fulfill the will of God in this life. I don't want to wait until I'm ninety to start doing the will of the Lord. While I can run, I'm going to run. While I have energy to pray through, I'm going to pray through. I want to be able to do whatever it is that God wants me to do, but I have to take these limitations off.

One thing that I've found is that sometimes our limitations don't come from other people. We put them on ourselves. There are times that nobody has said anything to us, but we're talking to ourselves. We start telling ourselves that we can't do certain things. God can send people to prophesy to us and bring us the Word of the Lord telling us what we are going to do, and we get excited. But when we get by ourselves, we question how in the world we are going to do what God said. We ask when we will be able to do it. We ask how we will be able to do it. We think those things are impossible. Then we go to another service and someone comes and tells us the same thing. We again ask God how we are going to do it because we have put limitations on ourselves.

John 5:19 & 30

"Then answered Jesus and said unto them, Verily, verily, I say unto you, The Son can do nothing of himself, but what he seeth the Father do: for what things soever he

doeth, these also doeth the Son likewise.....I can of mine own self do nothing: as I hear, I judge: and my judgment is just; because I seek not mine own will, but the will of the Father which hath sent me."

The key to you accomplishing the will of God is remembering that you can't do it by yourself anyhow. You have to set your eyes on Jesus. You can do everything you see Jesus do. I know we're gifted and talented. I know that we have it all going on and that we are all that and a bag of chips. That's nice, but guess what? That's not what qualifies you. What qualifies you is that you get in the presence of God and allow God to show you who you are. When He shows you who you are, He shows you what you can do. I'm reminded of the term "identity crisis." It has gotten so bad that we have moved from identity crisis to identity theft. "I can't be me, so I want to be you. If I can't be a good me, I want to be a better you. I'm gonna watch everything you do. I'm gonna act like you act. I'm gonna do what you do." I'm not saying that you won't receive attributes from others, but what I am saying is that there is a problem when you have nothing of your own. There is an issue when you don't even feel comfortable in your own skin because you don't even know what you like. We are given choices to make up our minds and we don't even know what we like because we have either stolen someone else's identity or we have lost our own.

When Jesus was talking back in the eighth chapter of John, He was setting a precedent. He was helping them to understand that sin was the problem. This is not about pointing fingers at your sins. The point is that when God delivered us from our sins, some of us still kept our sinful mindsets. It is like being sad about a baby you aborted twenty years ago even though you've been saved for twenty years. In your mind, you still feel low. In your mind, you're still telling yourself that God is not going to bless you because of what you did. You have to let that stuff go because that's not your identity anymore. That's who you were when you allowed sin to rule you, but now that you're in Jesus, all of that stuff is gone. We don't understand this. This is why the Scripture tells us in Romans 12:2 that we are supposed to be transformed by the renewing of our minds. As it says in 1 Peter 2:2: we must, *"desire the sincere milk of the word that we might grow thereby."* You have to drink this, you have to eat this, and you have to let this be your life. There is too much out here telling you that you are not and will never be who God says you are. We don't want to be restricted by any of these things.

Define: to give precise meaning to something including its nature or its basic or essential qualities, forms or properties; to determine the boundary or the extent of something. When people come to you and they try to define or redefine who you are, they are telling you what you have and that you don't have anything else. What they're telling you is that when they look at you, they don't see all of that extra stuff you're talking about. They don't see the calling of God on your life. They see the obstacles in your life that could prevent you from doing the will of God. The truth of the matter is that when God gets through with you, you will overcome every obstacle. You have to know that you can do whatever God says you can do. Yes, you had babies and had to put your life on hold for a second, and now you may be trying to figure out what's next. What's next is what was first all along - for you to be what God wants you to be. In order for you to do this, you have to look into the Word and see what the Word of God says.

One of the prerequisites of us being able to know who we are and walk in freedom is that we have to know the truth. I have experienced things that I just can't explain, and that's how I know that God is at work. When you are going through on the left and on the right and people are saying you did stuff when you weren't even there do to it... Nobody wants to give you the benefit of the doubt because they have already defined you. They accuse you and confirm the accusations without even asking you. Why? Because they already defined you. They have already determined what you are about and what your natures and qualities are. Unfortunately, we do that to each other all the time. We don't give each other a chance. We don't even understand that others could be carrying our deliverance and because we don't give them the chance to be who God created them to be, we cut ourselves off. We still have to walk around with our bondage and issues and problems not even knowing that we are sitting among treasures who could bring us the deliverance we need. We have to do better than that.

Colossians 3:3

"For ye are dead, and your life is hid with Christ in God."

I love the fact that Paul is trying to help them to understand just what was said in book of John. That old, simple stuff is not here anymore. Stop dwelling on that stuff. Paul let us know that we have already died and that our life "is hid with Christ in God." When I read that, God said to me: "You haven't even seen who you really are because I hid it. This is why you have to get in Me, so I can show you who you are. I don't care whose womb you came out of. I have to show you who you are because I hid it from you. I want you to come into my presence

18

and run after me with all that is in you so that I can show you who you really are." So what if they say that there are no women pastors. So what if they say that women can't preach? So what? Guess what? You don't define me. You can't confine me and you can't define me because my definition is in the Word of God. Whatever I see Jesus do, that's what I can do. Isn't that good stuff? You haven't seen you. You don't even know who you are. Because of that, we allow people to talk us out of destiny. We let people talk us out of stuff that God told us ions ago that we forgot about. I don't care who walks away from you. You have to know what God says to you. God want you to know who you are, and He doesn't want you to throw down your gifts or what He's anointed you to do because somebody else doesn't believe in you. Just as much as you believe in God, you're going to have to believe in yourself even if nobody else believes in you.

I John 3:2

"Beloved, now are we the sons of God, and it doth not yet appear what we shall be: but we know that, when he shall appear, we shall be like him; for we shall see him as he is."

I know that this is talking about the return of Christ, and as I said earlier, I am not going to exegete the text. However, there is still an appearing of Jesus before Jesus appears. It sounds like it doesn't make sense, but it does. He has to be seen in you first before the world can see Him and before He cracks the sky to come back to you. How in the world is that going to be possible if we're not looking at Him to see what He's doing? How is it that I'm going to be able to be what He is and see what He is and become everything that He's ordained for me to be when I'm letting somebody else tell me what I'm supposed to be. I'm not telling you to be in anarchy and to walk in rebellion. I'm not saying that. But I am saying to you that you're going to have to choose your company wisely. I remember Timothy Wright singing a song: "Jesus said if you go, I'll go with you. Open your mouth and I'll speak for you. Lord if I go, tell me what to say. They won't believe in me." That's what we're saying: "God how am I gonna go? These people aren't gonna believe me!" Listen here. If you have Jesus, the anointing speaks for itself. You don't have to speak anything about yourself. All you have to do is let Jesus speak. It goes back to what we were talking about before. It has nothing to do with your skill. It has nothing to do with your degrees. This is about you looking at Him when He appears, and not just in the sky. When you get a revelation of who Jesus is, and He begins to reveal to you all that He is and all that belongs to you, then you can do what He tells you that you are set here in this earth to do. You don't have to let anybody talk you out of it. Believe me, if it has never happened, keep

20

living. People will try to tell you that you're not called and that God didn't speak things to you. You may want to just go to the church and pray and they will make a big deal and ask you why you want to be in the church praying. They will say you are trying to deep. That is okay. There is some place in God that we need to be trying to get to. We should want to look like Jesus, sound like Jesus, smell like Jesus and be like Jesus. We should care who doesn't like it. People will call you a fanatic. Why is okay for you to be a baseball fan and a football fan and a golf fan but isn't not okay for me to be a Jesus fan? What's up with that? I will be a fan if I so choose to. Thank you, and I am.

Looking at those verses, you have to ask yourself some questions. Who am I? Who am I supposed to be? What do people say about me? Do I believe it? Do I believe what they're saying? Absolutely not, unless they're talking right. In this time that we are living in right now, I don't have any time to be playing around with people who are sure and unsure. I have enough issues by myself so I don't have time for your insecurities. My take: If you are not coming to fight... bye! It has to be that way. We're running out of time. You don't have any more time to sit here and ask yourself if you should be doing certain things that you know He told you to do. It's like being on a team and then waiting until the middle of the game to ask if you're supposed to be on the team. One thing that is so hilarious to me is that if we all did what Paul said concerning women being silent in the church (*1 Corinthians 13:34-35*) we would not have any church services. We wouldn't have anybody to lead prayer. We wouldn't have anybody to take up the offering. We wouldn't have anybody to come in an open the church. Who would clean the church? Because people doing right is so few and far between, who is going to pastor the church? If we want to take all of those crazy interpretations, we are in error. It is cultural. You have to know what happened before that lead up that verse. You have to know why he made that statement. You have to know what happened after the fact. You are not going to define me. I am going to be free to be me. I'm not being me like the world says; I am going to be everything that God says that I am. I am a royal priesthood and a chosen generation, and God has called me out of darkness and into His marvelous light (1 Peter 2:9). How can I carry that light if I'm sitting down being quiet? Jesus said that no man lights a candle and puts it under a bushel (Matthew 5:15), so let's cancel that one out. I'm not gonna sit here quiet, doing absolutely nothing, when I know I've been on my face seeking God. I'm not going to sit here knowing that God has been speaking to me and that He has given me something for someone else, and be quiet because someone else can't handle me being me. The devil is a liar! I need you to get this.

We have to do what God has said for us to do. I'm not saying that we run the brothers over. We are going to give space. I believe in biblical headship and I believe that it is right. But guess what? The Bible says that Christ is the head of the church (Ephesians 5:23), which means that He can put in charge whoever He wants to. He's the boss. He hires and fires. I want you (like Mary Mary said) to "take the shackles of your feet so you can dance." If you have a problem, then God bless ya! You have a problem. I don't have that problem because I took the time to see Jesus and when He appeared, I became what He is. Jesus could not help but to do what His Father did. It was a part of His nature to do what He saw His Father do. This is our real definition. Our basic qualities, our essential qualities, our form and our nature are all wrapped up in whom Jesus is. Everything that He is, we are. Why? Because He said so. I don't care if you're going through situations in your life, if someone is sick, if you're having problems with your children or in your marriage. Woman of God's get on your face and seek the Lord. God will answer your prayer just like He'll answer the prayer of a man.

I have to hit this hard because when you have a stronghold that is over a territory, it is called a stronghold for a reason. It's because nobody is taking the time to break it. That means that the stronghold has control of what goes in and what comes out of the city. What we need to do is ask God to break the strongholds off our cities so that the power of God can come in and so that we can see revival, healing and deliverances. We need to see people being set free by the power of God. If they say that we have to be quiet, let's be quiet long enough to get this prayer out. Some of us have gotten saved and people have beaten us down. When we first got saved, we were so zealous for God and we wanted to do things for Him. Then we started going through things and meeting people, and after a while that fire just started going out. You started losing that zeal because someone told you that what you were doing and saying didn't look right and sound right. It's okay to work on your presentation, but don't allow that to stop you from getting up and doing it again. Instead of bouncing back, we just shut down altogether. We let what others think or feel tell us whether or not we can be or do what God says.

We are in the hour where God has poured out His Spirit on all flesh (*Joel 2:28*), and as I say all the time: all means ALL. Brothers, just

24

deal with it, because all is all. If Jesus said I can do it, look out world because I'm coming. I saw Jesus do it and now I have a hunger for it. I've gotta do what I saw Him do. I can't help it. It's my nature. You have to be able to say the same thing. The more time you spend with God, the more you're going to be like Him. The world even has a saying that "association brings on assimilation." You are going to assimilate to whatever culture you submerge yourself in. If you sit around folks who don't believe in you and who tell you that you aren't good enough, you will not get past the place you are in. *"Faith without works is dead."* (James 2:17). The Bible says in 2 Corinthians 4:8 *"while we look not at the things which are seen, but at the things which are not seen; for the things which are seen are temporal, but the things which are not seen are eternal."* I'm not supposed to be looking at what is seen. My gain is supposed to be in heaven. I don't have any time to deal with what is going on in my street. For right now, I have an appointment, and I have to go spend time with Jesus so that He can show me where to go, what to do, and who to minister to. I have a people whose lives must be changed. First the Scripture says that Jesus is the light of the world *(John 8:12)* and then it comes back and says that ye are the light of the world *(Matthew 5:14)*. You're a light. A light does what a light does. It comes on. That's the nature of the bulb. When it connects with the electricity, it can't help but to come on. That's what it does. When you connect with Jesus who is your electricity and your life source, you can't help but to shine. You can't help it. If they get bad because you have the "can't help its", oh well. Now how is it that when we were in the world we didn't care about what anyone else thought of us? Now we try to say that us caring about what people thing is us trying to walk in love. Lies. You are letting people shut you down. You are letting people define you and redefine you. I'm free to be me, but who am I going to be? Am I going to be what others are saying, or am I going to go back to the Word and get my definition from the One who made me? He knows what He made me for. Picture me going over to one of these companies where they build things and I'm telling them that I don't want to use what they have for the purpose they made it for. Imagine me telling them that I want to use the chair they made as a bed. That's dumb. First of all, I would be uncomfortable. That chair is not created to be a bed; it's created to be a chair. That's the nature of it. That's what it was molded for. You were created and molded by God to fulfill the purpose that He created you for. Guess what? You've gotta do it. That nudging and gut-wrenching feeling you feel in your gut that keeps telling you to get up and do what God told you to do must be obeyed. That is God dealing with your heart. Even if people don't receive you, you must do it. What

I'm finding out is that the test of our faith lies in how we react to people receiving or not receiving us. We will do the will of God and witness to people and preach as long as we have a crowd. But what if you lose everything because of what you stand for? What if you lose your job? Now you have to believe God for income on top of doing what He told you to do. What if you lose your family behind following what God said? I found out that God will allow you to be humiliated in front of everybody and that everybody will be saying that you're down for the count. What I also found out is that when it looks like it's over, it's just getting started. As long as you have the promises of God, you can't quit. You can't quit! As long as you have God's Word, you have to keep going. I don't care if it looks upside down. I don't care if it looks like garbage. We have to deal with things about ourselves because we're too conscious of what people think of us.

What is real success? Success is sticking to whatever God gave you until what He told you comes to pass. Success is not about having a lot of money and having a good job. Being able to wait on God when things look contrary to what He said - that is success. Imagine how Moses felt when they were out in the wilderness of the wilderness with nothing but trees, rocks and dirt. All of the people were murmuring and complaining, and he had to figure out how to keep them encouraged so that they wouldn't kill him. People will be looking at you trying to figure out if God is really talking to you. There have been times when people have looked me in my face and told me that what I was saying wasn't God because of what was going on around me. I already told you that I do not care what is going on around me. I'm looking at eternity. I have to have an eternal gaze. When it pertains to your life, you have to look at what God has promised you and what He said you could be. You cannot give up on that. You have to have bulldog faith and bulldog tenacity. You cannot let anybody talk you out of what God said. Of course it's going to look contrary. When you're walking by faith, things look contrary. They questioned whether or not God was with the Apostle Paul when he was shipwrecked. They questioned whether or not God was with him when he went to jail. The Bible says that *"Indeed, all who desire to live godly in Christ Jesus will be persecuted."* (2 Timothy 3:2)" Your persecution can come in more than one form.

I want you to be encouraged and I want you to know that there is a plan that God has for you. If God has promised you anything, no matter what it is, you have to hold on to the promise. Hebrews 12:2 says that "for the joy that was set before him endured the cross, despising the

28

shame, and is set down at the right hand of the throne of God." Jesus endured His cross. He didn't care about the shame. He knew that He was going to have to be ashamed. I'm telling you that there are going to be times that you are going to have to bear your own shame even when you know what God is saying. Everybody else will be trying to say other stuff and talk you out of your promise. People will try to convince you otherwise, and this is why your identity must be sealed. You have to know that you know that you know. If you're going to accomplish the will of God, this is what you have to do. Ask yourself: What is everybody saying? Do I believe what they're saying or do I believe what the Word is saying? You've gotta get in the Word. You have to live in this Word. There are great things that God has and that He wants us to accomplish for Him. I want us as women of God of all ages to take the time to get a hold of God and get in His presence so that we can find out what is hidden. If someone has a gift for you and they hide it behind their back, you get up close because you want to see what they have for you. It should be the same with God. You are going to have to be intimate with God and spend time with Him so that He can show you what has been hidden from you in Him. He wants you to have what He hid. He wants you to be what was hidden so that you can show everybody who He really is.

Chapter Two

Warring for Your Future

I'm gonna tell you - you will get something out of the words in this section, but you have to pull on it. You have to pull on God if you want to receive what God has for you. This means that we have to be actively participating and not acting like we are watching a television show.

Let's go to Numbers 27:1-11 (English Standard Version):

Then drew near the daughters of Zelophehad the son of Hepher, son of Gilead, son of Machir, son of Manasseh, from the clans of Manasseh the son of Joseph. The names of his daughters were: Mahlah, Noah, Hoglah, Milcah, and Tirzah. And they stood before Moses and before Eleazar the priest and before the chiefs and all the congregation, at the entrance of the tent of meeting, saying, Our father died in the wilderness. He was not among the company of those who gathered themselves together against the Lord in the company of Korah, but died for his own sin. And he had no sons. Why should the name of our father be taken away from his clan because he had no son?

Give to us a possession among our father's brothers. Moses brought their case before the Lord.

And the Lord said to Moses, The daughters of Zelophehad are right. You shall give them possession of an inheritance among their father's brothers and transfer the inheritance of their father to them. And you shall speak to the people of Israel, saying, 'If a man dies and has no son, then you shall transfer his inheritance to his daughter. And if he has no daughter, then you shall give his inheritance to his brothers. And if he has no brothers, then you shall give his inheritance to his father's brothers. And if his father has no brothers, then you shall give his inheritance to the nearest kinsman of his clan, and he shall possess it. And it shall be for the people of Israel a statute and rule, as the Lord commanded Moses.'"

We are reading in this passage of Scripture about Zelophehad who was a descendant of Manasseh. Manasseh was a son of Joseph. Zelophehad died and when he died, he left his daughters (he had no sons). We are tearing down the walls and we are taking the limits off of God. We are women of God warring for our future. In this Scripture, it is important for you to understand that this man had no sons. In a patriarchal society where men ruled everything and the women were subservient to the men, if the father had no son, when he died, his daughters would become poor. They would be reliant on aid from other people. What I love about this is that these women did not stick with the law. Have you ever challenged the law? You know what it says, you know that they are telling you what you can't do, but there is something on the inside that tells you that there has to be more. Something on the inside of you tells you that you have a right to war for your future.

These women get together and they say, "Wait a minute. We know that we don't have a brother. Our father didn't have any sons. But this is not right that we are going to have to give up his land and lose our inheritance." Now these ladies had a lot of stuff going against them. The fact that they were women was just one strike. The first thing that was really the most important problem was that they were of the tribe of Manasseh. They were of the half-tribe. Manasseh was only a half-=tribe. There were two half-tribes: Ephraim and Manasseh, which were the children of Joseph's Egyptian wife. What this meant was that they only had half a right to an inheritance. So here I have half a right to an inheritance and then now my daddy is dead, and now you're telling me that I have NO right to an inheritance? The devil is a liar. So these women were stirred up in their spirits and they said, "We are gonna go stand before the man of God, and we're going to ask him about this law." Verse two says, "And they stood before Moses and before Eleazar the priest and before the chiefs and all the congregation, at the entrance of the tent of meeting, saying, (3) 'Our father died in the wilderness. He was not among the company of those who gathered themselves together against the Lord in the company of Korah...'" Let's stop right there. Do you know the story of Korah? Korah challenged Moses, and because of his rebellion, the Bible says that the earth opened up and swallowed him and his company whole (Numbers 16:32) because he was rebellious. These women were smart. Even with us - when you go to God, you had better know what you know. You had better know God's Word, and if you want Him to move, you have to come to Him correct. You have to come to God according to His Word. Here they were saying, "Look. Y'all are judging us, but let me tell you that our father was a righteous man. He did not rebel against the man of God when Korah rebelled against the man of God." In this verse where it says that he died for his own sin (verse three), that word in the Hebrew really means that he separated himself from sin, so this is not a good translation. Really, what they are saying is that their father was holy and that he separated himself from sin.

Now, here's a little sidebar: If you want God to move for you, you can't be living in sin. If you want God to move for you, you are going to have to get sin out of your life. Now I know that we have problems, situations, and stuff that we are going through. I know that we have things we have been struggling with. I'm not talking about stuff you're trying to get delivered from. I'm talking about stuff you're having fun engaging in. Women of God warring for their future. Verse four says, "Why should the name of our father be taken away from his clan because he had no son?" In essence, what they were saying nicely was, "Moses, that's a dumb law." That's what they were saying. "This doesn't make any sense. What do you mean? We're gonna lose our land and our place in society because we don't have a brother? " Verse four continues to say, "Give to us a possession among our father's brothers." This is what I love.

Let's continue reading: "Moses brought their case before the Lord. And the Lord said to Moses, "The daughters of Zelophehad are right. You shall give them possession of an inheritance among their father's brothers and transfer the inheritance of their father to them."

34

Let me help you understand why this was such a time of rejoicing for them. Number one, Zelophehad was the firstborn son of Manasseh, which means, "wound". I want you to pay attention to these names. His name also means, "captured" or "to be taken". What you have to understand is that any time you see a name in Scripture, it's a prophecy over that person's life. So whenever they were named something, it was God speaking their destiny. So here we have Zelophehad whose name was "wound" or "captured" or "to be taken captive," which means that he was subject to being bound. He lived a life of bondage. That's what his problem was. He was of the half-tribe. He was a man, but he was in bondage. Have you ever been bound? That's not fun.

So then he had a daughter. His firstborn's name was Mahlah, which meant "sickly, weak and diseased". Her name also means, "wound". What that meant is that there was a generational curse. We talk about fighting for our future, but let's remember that if you are going to fight for your future, you have to deal with your past. You have to deal with the things that mama and grandma did. You have to deal with all that sin that has caused you to walk in bondage and keep you from getting free. You have to recognize that the devil just wants you to think you're just going in circles and having problems. He doesn't want you to know that it's deeper than that. It's deeper than that. This is stuff that is rooted in generations. This is why these women were having problems. They were women (not men), and when people called their names, they knew that they had problems. Now you know folks that come around you and as soon as you call their name, you already know. People tell you not to call them and when they are called, the response is: "Oh Lord, here he/she comes." You know how people do. It was the same thing with these names.

The second daughter was named Noah which means "motion, waiver, stagger" or "cursed to wander". Do you get it? Generational curses perpetuating themselves over the lives of these women who had set in their hearts that they were not going to be moved. What was her problem? She was unstable. She was suffering from a vagabond spirit even though she had a father. She couldn't be still. She was moving from one place to the other place. She couldn't get stable because her name (the prophecy over her) said that she was unstable. What am I telling you? I'm telling you that if you want to be free you have to deal with the prophecy that is over your life. God has spoken one thing, but the enemy and your bloodline said something else. You can walk around here acting like the devil has no power all you like. If the devil had no power, how come it took us so long to get saved? It wasn't just because we were having a good time in the world. It's because he blinded us and we couldn't see.

The next daughter was named Hoglah, which meant "partridge". It took me a few minutes to try to understand what this meant. In other words, when she was named, they named her after the personality of a bird. A partridge is a bird that sets its nest on the ground, which is not smart. What happens to the eggs when they are laid? In other words, she was unwise and she didn't make good decisions. We have all struggled with bad decision-making.

The next daughter was Milcah, which means "counselor", "Queen appointed to reign, set up, or consulted". This is where somebody has some sense when they started naming these children. Somebody said, "I wanna be delivered." Sometimes you learn from this other kids and realize that you must name the other child something else because things aren't working. The Bible says that we will have whatsoever we say (Mark 11:23). So if we say something and it keeps manifesting, there is no need for us to keep asking

37

ourselves why we are still in a rut. You are in a rut because of what you keep saying.

The last daughter's name was Tirzah whose name means "benevolent, pleasant, favorable or to be accepted". So here we saw in the end that God was setting them up to be favorable and accepted even though they were born to be rejected. I want you to know that I don't care what your mother said. I don't care what they named you or how many names they called you. I don't care what they said about your behavior and your physical appearance. We are going to war for our future, and we are not accepting anything that the devil says. I have had enough of the enemy prophesying over me and trying to tell me what I'm going to be and what I can and cannot do. I will do everything that God says I will do. I don't care if my mother was a whore. I don't care if she was married five times. I don't care if none of us have the same daddy. That has nothing to do with me because my God is strengthening me to be able to war for my future. I don't care who's dying. I don't care who's rebelling. I'm warring for my future. I'm not going anywhere, and neither are you, until you finish everything God put in you to do. You have to have that kind of resolve. You can bury your whole family but you better know that you aren't going anywhere until God says so. I am not playing with the devil. I am warring for my future. What you have to understand that this isn't just about you. This is about your seed. This is why when we look at these verses, we see that from one generation to the next, we went from one wound to the next. Daddy was hurt, now I'm hurt. Now I have babies and my babies are hurt. The devil is a liar. We are going to speak life over our seed. They are going to live and not die. They are going to walk in the Spirit, hear in the Spirit, see in the Spirit and live in the Spirit. So am I. I don't care if they are acting right stupid. Don't they act stupid? I don't care what they do. They can turn their bodies inside out, dye their hair four shades of purple, and go get every body part pierced... They can go sleep with him, her, them or that... I am warring for my future.

I am trying to get you stirred up because for too long, we have accepted our circumstances. For too long we have allowed the enemy to run over us and we say that whatever we have to go through is what we have to go through. The devil is a liar. It is time for you to start prophesying over your house. It's time for you to start prophesying over your husband. It's time for you to start prophesying over your child, over your marriage, and over your checkbook. These girls realized that what their father worked for was worth more than whatever the Law said. We have to get to the point where we start taking no for an answer. I don't care if you've been praying four years for someone to be saved. Stay on your face. God is not a man that He should lie, neither the son of man that He should repent (Numbers 23:19). If you do like these women did and go right... You have to have some type of godly history that you can pull up. He said that if we keep His commandments, then He knows that we love Him (John 14:21). So how are we going to get God to move for us when He doesn't even know that we love Him because we aren't doing what He said? We're doing what we want to do. How many times do we do what we want to do? How many times do we do what GOD wants us to do? We are too wrapped up in whatever our situations are. These girls had issues. We think we have issues, but these girls had issues. It's one thing for you to have a whole family and only certain ones have problems. They were ALL jacked up except for two. They were all basket cases except for two. Thank God for the two. God will never leave Himself without a witness. Your whole family might be jacked up, but you're not. They all might be unsaved, but you're not. You are going to have to do some warfare for them who don't know how to war for themselves. The thing about it is that these women were pushing against societal trends. They were pushing against tradition. I have had people question me. "You're a woman and you're an apostle? Where does the Bible say that?" Guess what? I show them the Scripture, and if they don't believe it, tough kitty paws. Them having questions has nothing to do with me. I'm pushing against tradition. I'm pushing against tradition because this is what God said. If God said it, Amen. Bless you. That's what you have to say. That's the way you have to be. You cannot allow anything in this life to dictate to you what you're going to do for God. This is what we forget. We are thinking that we're human trying to master this experience, but God wants us to be able to master this experience walking in the Spirit twenty-four hours a day, seven days a week. There's a place God wants us to walk in where we're not tripping and falling. In this place, we won't be falling in sin, making mistakes and falling in bondage of the same sin over and over and over again. God is a deliverer. If you believe Him for deliverance, He will deliver you. I am a living witness. I used to be a smoker. I smoked everything that could burn. I sniffed it; I smoked it... because I thought I was grown. I had it bad. I thought I was really grown until those things started to kill me. I thank God for His mercy, and I thank Him for deliverance.

When I got saved, I was living people who were religious but not saved. I thank God for them allowing me to live in their house. After I got saved, I got kicked out because if I wasn't going to go to the Methodist church I couldn't live there. That's what they told me. "We are Methodist, and if you aren't going to be Methodist, you have to go." They wanted to know what all of this speaking in tongues stuff was. They thought it was crazy. I was going to church at their church and crying, and they thought I had problems. They didn't know that it was the Spirit of God. I went on a three-day fast when I first got saved and the Lord took the taste of cigarettes out of my mouth. It wasn't from anybody laying hands or prophesying over me. I'm trying to tell you that if you go after God, you will find Him. That's the kind of God we serve. He wants you to encounter Him by yourself so that nobody else can take the credit.

Going back to these ladies: They decided that they were going to fight against tradition. They also decided that they were going to fight against the curse that was on their bloodline. They always saw the inability to have a son as a curse. This means that in their minds, their mother was cursed and their father was cursed. That's sad. That's "bad business". They were having babies but they weren't having the right thing. That has spiritual implications. We have babies but we don't have the right thing.

Here is what these ladies did. Number one, they united as one for the cause. Who said that women can't get along with each other and that we always have to be cat fighting and bickering and gossiping? The devil is a liar. They broke that curse. They said, "We are going to come together because we're gonna get this land." They could have been stoned for going to Moses and Eleazar and all of the priests and challenging the law. How bold are you? One thing I find is that we are bold when we are mad and have an attitude. But can we be bold just for general purposes? Can you just be bold because that's who God called you to be and not just because somebody riled you up? You should walk in a spirit of boldness because you know who you are and whose you are. If you are suffering with identity crisis, we will deal with that as well. Dr. Jesus is in the building. You are not going to have to take a pill to get rid of any psychotic situations - He will deliver you by Himself.

Number two, they waited for the right time. They talked amongst themselves about how the land belonged to them and how they were not going to give it up. They talked about how they were cursed, how their parents were cursed, and how they didn't have any brothers. They talked about how they didn't have anybody whom they could rely on to fight for them, but that no matter what, they were not giving up the land. They had a mentality like Esther. They believed that whatever it took, they were going to get results. You have to have a spiritual resolve like that. This is why the enemy is so easily able to speak to us and talk us out of our destiny. We don't have any resolve. We feel good while we are in church, but when we go home, we are crying and sobbing to Jesus. We need help! When we get home, we should have the same resolve, the same fire, and the same fervor that we had when we were in church. That fire you feel is not reserved for a building. It should be with you every day.

The next thing they did was they made their appeal. One of the things that the Lord was speaking to me was that they have this television show called "Snapped". The show is usually about women who had all they could take and they snapped. I wish somebody would "snap" in the Holy Ghost. I wish somebody would get tired of the devil and snap in the Spirit. Then we would be able to slay some demons. Then you might really get some deliverance that lasts because you snapped. We like watching that because it's entertaining, but what we really need to see is that these ladies have reached their breaking point. The reason that the devil is still having a heyday with you is because you aren't really tired. You say you're tired, but you're not really tired.

We have to fight for this. I want to reference Matthew 11:12 which says, "From the days of John the Baptist until now the kingdom of heaven has suffered violence, and the violent take it by force." You aren't getting anything talking about "Please Mr. Devil... Mr. Devil please give me my stuff..." He is not thinking about you. The violent take it by force. I'm going to tell you something. I learned something having children. I thought I was patient, but children will try you. They will try to get you to snap the wrong way. I have four children, and they have all tried me. I have snapped a couple of times the wrong way and I had to ask the Lord to forgive me. I love young people, but my Savior... I'm learning how to just smile while they're cutting the fool and acting like demon-filled people. Why? Because I'm warring. Do you remember the commercial where they used to say, "Never let them see you sweat"? I'm sweating, but you won't know it. I'm crying, but you don't know it. You keep messing with me and I'm right there about to snap - but I'm talking about in the Holy Ghost. We are going

45

to mess around and give God that forty-day fast. We're going to mess around and really give it to Him, because that's really what He wants. On that forty-day fast He can really kill you. We worry about natural death, but God is not thinking about that. He just wants to kill your flesh.

I'm excited about Jesus because I already know that from the position we are fighting from, we are already victorious. Let me tell you something. Just because you're fighting and you get mad and start crying doesn't mean you're a wimp. That's just an emotional thing. You can cry but still fight. Don't let my tears fool you. My tears don't mean I gave up. My tears don't mean that I'm turning around or that I've turned my back on God. It just means that I'm crying. Women, we have to have a resolve. You know how we used to do (some of us still do this and need to be delivered): we tie up our wig and pull those combs out and get ready to fight. Why do we fight dirty in the world and come to church and become wimps? I'm taking prisoners. I'm taking hostages. They have something in piracy called the booty, which is the treasure - I'm going to get it. I've cried too much and I'm sick of this mess. I'm sick and tired of being sick and tired. I have told my kids, "Go ahead and do what you're doing. I love you. I'm praying for you. By the way, you're going to be saved. You're just trying to figure out where you belong because the enemy is playing games." The devil messed around and let me find this Scripture. I'm challenging the Law. I don't care what they say. The Law says that the wages of sin is death, but it also says that the gift of God is eternal life through Jesus Christ (Romans 6:23). Guess what? The Law also says that "The effectual fervent prayer of a righteous man availeth much" (James 5:16).

I read the word and once I find it, if you can gook it you can live it. Not only can you live it but you can claim it. Not only can you claim it, but you can also go to God and remind Him that He said it. Let's go to Ezekiel 12:28 - " Therefore say to them, Thus says the Lord God: None of my words will be delayed any longer, but the word that I speak will be performed, declares the Lord God." If you were really believing God for something, that is where you should have praised Him. This is the deal about being in a season of birthing. They have assistance for mothers who are having a hard time pushing the babies out. It's called induced labor. When you are holding on to stuff for too long, God knows how to induce your labor. He knows how to get that baby out of your belly. You cannot be pregnant for too long. The baby will die and so can you. So therefore the Lord says that the season is no longer prolonged. Your nine months are up. They are up! You might as well get your feet in the stirrups, take a shower, and get your hospital gown on. Let's get ready. You've got to have this baby. You have to go against the grain. You have to war in the season to have what God has called you to have. It is not going to just come to you on a silver platter. We already know that we are seated in heavenly places in Christ Jesus (Ephesians 2:6) but the warfare is really realizing that you're seated in heavenly places in Christ Jesus. I looked up the word for "priest" and the word is synonymous with "war". Do you want to be a leader? You are going to have to be in war. I heard someone say that serving is warfare and warfare is service. I never understood what they were saying, but that is some heavy stuff right there. You are not going to be able to get anything without warring. Everything that you get, the Kingdom of heaven suffers violence, and the violent take it by force. Even though the season is no longer prolonged, you still have to be able to discern your season. It's a crazy woman that will carry a baby and not know how long she's been pregnant. Loose here. Especially in the summer - the devil is a liar. I've been there: fat, hot, sweaty - that is not God. You have to realize that what God has given you is worth fighting for. I don't care what came down through your bloodline. It stops here. I had to show this to my children. My brother was on his deathbed at thirty-four years old with congestive heart failure. Normally I would just say that I would pray, but I felt an urgency in my spirit to go. We went down there and prayed with him and decreed life over him. We decreed that he would live and not die because I knew that this was a generational curse. How did I know? Because my grandmother, my uncle and my mother died from congestive heart failure. My brother, my sister and I are the only ones left from my mother's bloodline. My uncle has one child left from his bloodline. So I'm familiar with what they were saying. I had to go down there and sit down and open the Word and explain to him what generational curses were. I had to explain to him that he had to get under the blood and that he could not afford not to be saved. I told him that he wasn't going to be able to just will himself better because there was a demonic spirit that was attached to him in the womb. That's what generational curses are about: demonic spirits that have been attached in the womb to follow you all of your life and to wreak havoc in your life. They are designed to cause you to be miserable and pining over whatever issues your bloodline has had. We went down there and he was in full congestive heart failure in the intensive care. I laid hands on him, I prayed for him, I rebuked death off of him, and I told him that

49

he was going to live and not die. I came against the generational curse and declared that it stops here. I have power because it stops here. I don't care if momma died from congestive heart failure. Uncle died, sorry. Grandma died, and I'm sorry about that too. My heart aches. One of my sisters was murdered and that is a whole different spirit. There are only three of my mother's four children left. I told him that he would not die right then. We prayed for him and prayed for him. I anointed him. I laid my prayer shawl on him and told him that he was going to live. In two days, they took him out of intensive care and put him in a regular room. He was still having issues because at night, a spirit was attacking him and snatching his breath out of his body. They thought he'd had a heart attack and they wanted to perform a lot of tests. The Lord spoke to me and told me that it was a spirit of torment and for me to go in the room. I got someone to watch the kids and I went and stayed in the hospital room all night. I spoke the Word of the Lord over him. I rebuked the spirit of death that was coming to torment him and to snatch his life. Brother man is alive with a clean bill of health. He is not in congestive heart failure anymore. You have to understand that your future is about your seed and everybody connected to. This is why we don't have time to be playing church. We don't have time for religious games. This is for real for real. If you have never seen for real for real, welcome to the park. This right here is the real deal. We don't have time to be playing. You'd better get some power with God. Shouting is wonderful, but what is on the inside. Is your spirit on empty and you're just shouting because you feel good? It is time for us to war for our future because God said that His words would not be prolonged anymore. I don't care who has backslidden. I don't care who is living in raunchy sin. Some of my kids are living in raunchy sin. Heartbreaking sin. Sin that I cried over, asking God what in the world was going on. I fasted while I was pregnant and laid hands on them. The Lord told me to keep speaking over them. I know that if God brought me out with my crazy self (used to be), I am waiting for Him to do the same for my seed. I'm waiting for Him to do it for my sister and for my brother. I remember my brother calling me crying and saying that something happened to him that particular morning. He said that he got up to pray and he was just going to pray for a few minutes, but he started crying and couldn't stop. He said that he started thinking about all the things he did to God and all the times he turned his back on God. He said that he thought about all the times that he had played games and the times he told God that he was going to do right but he didn't do it. He wasn't in church when he had this experience. He was at home. We were praying (when he was sick) that God wouldn't just heal his body but that He would heal his soul. What good is it for him to walk away healed but continue in sin? He kept me on the phone for an hour. He cried and cried. He apologized for holding me up and he said he didn't know what happened. I told him that it was God and that it was the answer to prayer. I told him that it was the spoil coming in from war. I'm not going to be battling and not take any hostages. Read your Bible. When the Israelites went in and took control of a land, they took the gold, the silver and the cattle. You're going to have to go in and take what belongs to you and then some. It's called interest. Yes, I want it. The Bible says that if a thief steals, he has to give you back what he stole with interest. You have to know what the Word says. No more delaying. No more playing games. No more looking at what someone else is doing. No more worrying about how somebody else might feel about you.

You have got to soar. You have got to come above your life's circumstances. You have got to come above what you're thinking, how you feel, what people said, how people feel about you, what your mother said about you, and even how you feel about you. Some of our own feelings about ourselves are not healthy. Some of us don't love ourselves like we should. The Bible tells us in Mark 12:31 to love our neighbors as we love ourselves. I'm not talking about having pride, but you should have a healthy love for yourself knowing that God loves you. It should drive you to take care of yourself.

I want you to begin to renounce the things that you have been struggling with. I want you to give up all of that stuff. I want you to let go of everything that has been holding you back. Let go of even the fear of moving on. Let go of the fear of letting go. You can't be afraid of heights right here. You have soar above your problems and your circumstances.

Chapter Three

I Will Not Be Denied!

The people of God are facing challenges like never before. The fire has gotten hotter. There has been a strange spirit of testing that has been released. We call it strange but the Bible tells us in 1 Peter 4:12: "Dear friends, don't be surprised at the fiery trials you are going through, as if something strange were happening to you." We always say that people are trying us, but I am finding out that God has been trying us too. The Lord has been trying us, and I'm so glad that He saw fit to try me. I've been meditating on Psalm 8:4 which says, "What is man, that thou art mindful of him? and the son of man, that thou visitest him?" What is it about us that concerns God that He had to stop what He was doing to send us a savior? What is it about us that He would assign angels to go before us and prepare a way before we get here? What is it about us that He would sit on the circle of the earth and decree a thing for us? Who is it that we are in His sight that He's so concerned and loves us so much? I don't know about you but that just baffles me. It makes me feel good at the same time, but I'm just baffled by His love.

Let's look at Numbers 26:33 & 55-56 (KJV):

"And Zelophehad the son of Hepher had no sons, but daughters: and the names of the daughters of Zelophehad were Mahlah, and Noah, Hoglah, Milcah, and Tirzah. Notwithstanding the land shall be divided by lot: according to the names of the tribes of their fathers they shall inherit. According to the lot shall the possession thereof be divided between many and few."

I need you to see this because sometimes we get stuck in a time warp and we don't understand that God is a God of equity. When you read this chapter, you see that the children of Israel are about to go into the Promised Land, but there is a family that has a problem. The problem is the Law. Not only is it the Law, but it's also God - because God is the author of the Law. One thing I'm finding out is that sometimes it seems like God will decree something that seems like a total oxymoron and a paradox. It seems that it has no bearing over what He is supposed to be speaking to us. Here we are looking at the fact that this man had only daughters, which meant that there were no sons. This means that even though everybody was getting their inheritance, his daughters were getting nothing.

Let's go over to Numbers 27:1-11 (KJV)

"Then came the daughters of Zelophehad, the son of Hepher, the son of Gilead, the son of Machir, the son of Manasseh, of the families of Manasseh the son of Joseph: and these are the names of his daughters; Mahlah, Noah, and Hoglah, and Milcah, and Tirzah. And they stood before Moses, and before Eleazar the priest, and before the princes and all the congregation, by the door of the tabernacle of the congregation, saying, Our father died in the wilderness, and he was not in the company of them that gathered themselves together against the Lord in the company of Korah; but died in his own sin, and had no sons. Why should the name of our father be done away from among his family, because he hath no son? Give unto us therefore a possession among the brethren of our father. And Moses brought their cause before the Lord. And the Lord spake unto Moses, saying, The daughters of Zelophehad speak right: thou shalt surely give them a possession of an inheritance among their father's brethren; and thou shalt cause the inheritance of their father to pass unto them. And thou shalt speak unto the children of Israel, saying, If a man die, and have no son, then ye shall cause his inheritance to pass unto his daughter. And if he have no daughter, then ye shall give his inheritance unto his brethren. And if he have no brethren, then ye shall give his inheritance unto his father's brethren. And if his father have no brethren, then ye shall give his inheritance unto his kinsman that is next to him of his family, and he shall possess it: and it shall be unto the children of Israel a statute of judgment, as the Lord commanded Moses."

These verses are loaded. There are several things going on in this chapter. As I began to read, I understood the saying they have in the world: "Favor rests on the bold." It takes a boldness for you to get some things that you will get in this life. I once went through one of the hardest tests I have ever had to face. I still had to stand up and preach like a superwoman. I was thinking about this as a check and a balance for myself. As I began to look at where I was that particular year and then look at where I am today, having to make some decisions that I didn't have to make and stand in some places I would rather not stand in, I realize that God orchestrates opposition. God began to deal with me about orchestrated opposition. You see trouble and turmoil and the hell you're going through. You see that trauma you're dealing with and the trials you have to face. You see the people getting on your nerves. Stuff is shutting down on you. Doors are closing on you. Things that aren't supposed to be coming open aren't coming open. There are things God is allowing you to face in public that you wish He would allow you to face in private. Yet, God is saying that He orchestrated all of this opposition. As I looked at these women the Lord spoke to me and said, "It was Me who gave their father only daughters. It was Me who gave Moses the law and said that only men (and not just men, but the firstborn) could receive the inheritance. It was also Me who stirred them up and told them that they didn't have to settle for what was being told to them." There's something on the inside of me that tells me that I'm supposed to have more. I've been sitting back watching everybody else get their promise while I'm sitting on the edge of my promised land. Do you mean to tell me that I'm going to watch everybody else get what God said and then not get mine? I refuse to be denied! I don't care what the Law says. I'm going to go to God and He's going to work this out on my behalf.

I began to look at these women and God reminded me that He orchestrated it all. He was setting them up because He wanted to show everybody that He's still God. If God gave the Law then God can change the Law. God said, "It was also Me who stood with them as they stood before Eleazar and Moses and entreated Moses concerning their inheritance. It was Me who favored them. In the end, it was still me who gave them justice." God is a God of equity. I don't care what seems unfair right now. Life isn't always fair. We complain about it feeling like God is leaving us out and that we aren't getting everything that's due us. We feel like God has left us out. We talk about how long we've been crying and worrying. We reminisce about how we have looked like a fool in front of everybody else, who people have pointed their fingers and whispered about us, and how we have gone through for so long. "What's wrong with You, God? Why have you set me up like this?" we say. God responds with, "I'm a God of justice and equity."

Let's go back and look at these ladies. God began to deal with me about who they were and what they were experiencing. These women were smart. Nowhere in the Scripture does it say that they fought for their place. We don't like for people to touch our stuff. We always have to speak up for ourselves because in our minds, if we don't speak up for ourselves, nobody else will. What these ladies did was that they got together. Let's nip this in the bud that women can't work together. The devil is a liar. These women proved that we can put aside our egos and how we feel, and that we could go ahead and get the job done.

Let's look at the names of Zelophehad's daughters: Mahlah, Noah, Hoglah, Milcah and Tirzah. You already know when we see names, that is a prophetic sign about what God is speaking about that person and their personality. There is a positive side and a negative side. Let's talk about Mahlah. Mahlah must have been a tiny baby when she was born because her mother named her "weak and sickly". When we get to Noah, we see that the man's name in Genesis means "rest or comfort," but her name means, "that that quivers or totters". She was mentally unstable and couldn't get it together. Hoglah's name means "partridge, cricket, grasshopper or locust". When you look up her name, you will also see that it means "house of birds". The partridge is a bird that is fearful. It runs away and it cries out loud constantly. The partridge also means "unstable". In essence, she was a child who got on her mother's nerves because she cried too much. All she did was cry, and as a child, she didn't deal with circumstances because she was always running from something. She was always fearful and unstable. Her next sister's name is Milcah, which means "queen" or "bossy" or "someone who has a strong personality".

Today's translation would be that she was a diva. She was full of attitude and nobody could deal with her because her stronghold was pride. Then you have Tirzah. Tirzah is "the pleasant one". Her name means, "to be favored, received or accepted". She was the good child. She was the one who didn't give her mother any problems. She was a good pregnancy and an easy delivery. She was a quiet baby and everybody loved her. She wanted to please everybody. This could be a problem because behavior like this often turns people into man pleasers when they should be God pleasers.

As I began to look at this, the Lord began to speak to me and show me that these are the issues that we have to deal with while we are saying that God is going to use us. Sometimes we have to deal with the fact that we are weak people who can't take anything. Sometimes you have physical ailments that get in the way of you walking out and being obedient to what God has called you to do. We are fearful at times. What would you do if you weren't afraid? There things that God has spoken to us and put in our hearts to do but because we are afraid, we don't do them. I know good and well that we have some stuff that we're afraid of. The first thing we do when God speaks to us is question if it's even God speaking to us. Some of us are crybabies.

We are always crying about something. People get the tissue in advance because they already know. You can't keep running from your circumstances. When you get to wherever it is that you're running to, you are still going to be with you. That means that you will still have to deal with you.

These ladies had to put away all of their personal isms and schisms. They had to deal with being bossy, being weak, and how they interacted with each other. They had to deal with the weak ones telling the bossy ones that they talked too much and the bossy ones telling the weak ones to step up and say something. They were dealing with all of this personal stuff. We're not even talking about what was going on on the outside. Everybody on the outside already knew that the daughters weren't entitled to anything. Everybody was already talking and trying to figure out what Moses was going to do with Zelophehad's portion. They knew what the Law said, and they knew that the women weren't supposed to get anything. Let me hit a stronghold right quick. I will preface what I'm about to say by saying that I am not a "man hater". I rebuke that spirit. I have learned personally through my own opposition that there is a stronghold in the Carolinas that causes men to have their foot on women. Some of us when faced with situations like this would just grin and bear it. We would just say, "Oh well... That's what the Law says, and we can't mess with the Law." Now one of the things I like is that in the natural we know that we can go and petition our government and sit before them in an effort to get them to change laws. God began to show me that these women had the gall to go before God and petition Him so that He would change His law. If you are bold enough, God will change His mind just because you asked. "No" is not always the final answer. You have to be able to say, "'No' is not what I'm taking because I know what God said!" Those ladies didn't bother fighting with the other tribes because the other tribes really didn't have a say in it. God orchestrated this opposition and since He orchestrated it, we have to deal with Him. They had to be bold. They told each other, "Listen here: you stop that crying, and you stop that talking. You don't go up there looking like you're scared. Hold my hand if you have to hold my hand, but we're going in there together and we're going to seek God for what He wants for us! This is our inheritance and we will not settle for less than what's mine. I will not watch it be given to someone else." The devil is a liar. If I have to go to God and beg Him to change His mind, He has to change His mind for me.

This is a sidebar: When you go back to Genesis you will see that Noah got off the ark and offered a sacrifice unto the Lord. Some of us think that it wasn't until Jesus got here that dominion was reinstated. If you go back to the Word, the Bible says that the offering that Noah offered to the Lord smelled so good that God changed His mind and cut another covenant. He reinstated the promise that He gave to Adam in the beginning. When I saw that, it helped me to see that this is just what God does. It's His nature. It doesn't mean that God is double-minded. It means that God is looking for someone who is bold enough to enter into His presence. He's looking for someone who believes Him enough to say "God I need You to do this for me." These girls learned that if they couldn't get what the needed on their own, they would legislate on their knees. They knew that they could go to God and ask God to turn this thing around for them. They weren't gonna watch anybody else walk off with their stuff.

Yes I'm going through hell. Yeah they're talking. Yes they've written all over Facebook and all over social media. I don't care! I'm still not going to let anybody else walk off with my stuff. I understand that it's God who has orchestrated this opposition. He was waiting to see if you still believed. He was waiting to see if you still would trust

Him. He was waiting to see if you still wanted what He said. He is saying, "Can you believe that I'm still with you and that I'm still God?" Mahlah could have said, "I don't feel good. I'm sick. I can't go. Y'all go for me today. I just feel weak. My back hurts, my neck hurts, my head hurts, and I don't feel like going." But her sisters wouldn't let her sit back in her sickness. Sometimes you are going to have to grab your sister by the hand and say, "I don't care what you're dealing with. I need you to be thinking about the promise that God has given to you. I need for you to be reminded that God is not a man that He should lie. I need you to remember that everything God spoke will come to pass. He knows how to make His word good." And if that wasn't enough, go back into the verses and read. If you look at verse three, the daughters are saying that really their father should be disqualified because he messed up in the end. But guess what? He didn't mess up like the rest of them.

We have all jacked up stuff. We have all lost our tempers and said things that we shouldn't have said. We have all felt things we shouldn't have felt. All of the above. But when it came down to the rebellion, we have to make sure that we don't rebel against Him. This is when we can remind God of His promise. If we just walk in repentance and ask God to forgive us and help us, we will see the manifestation. Learn how to just get over you. It's not what someone else is saying. It doesn't matter to me what anyone else is saying. It's about what's going on up here in my mind. Do I feel like I'm sick? Do I feel like I'm weak? Do I feel like I'm going run or quit or give up? Or am I standing on the Word of God? Sometimes you have to talk yourself back into the promises of God.

These girls were out of this world. They had it going on. They weren't scared. Sometimes we have to do like they used to say in the commercial: "Never let them see you sweat." I may be sweating pork and bean juice, but I'm not about to let you know. I'll go in the bathroom and get a rag and wipe it off, and I'm coming back out. I'm going to stand up before Moses. I'm going to stand before Eleazar, and I am going to petition for what's mine. Why? Because God orchestrated this opposition.

My mind goes to the New Testament. The wilderness is all about questioning you. The wilderness is all about understanding your identity in God. The wilderness is all about you being secure in who you are. When Jesus went in to the wilderness (Matthew 4), the Bible says that He was tempted because He had fasted forty days and forty nights. When the enemy came to Him to tempt Him, the only thing the devil said was "If thou be the Son of God then why don't you..." That's what I'm finding out. The devil will try to put you on blast to try to make you prove who you are. I don't have anything else to prove but what is that good, acceptable and perfect will of God (Romans 12:2). If they don't believe me for my word's sake, they will have to believe me for THE WORD'S sake. I don't have time to try to prove to you who I am. You will have to get a revelation from God. If you can't believe that I went before God and He changed His mind on my behalf, then guess what? You weren't supposed to be with me in the first place. You weren't supposed to walk beside me in the first place. You weren't supposed to be my friend in the first place. That's why it's called "the revelation of Jesus Christ". It has to be revealed. Jesus knew what He was saying when He told Peter that flesh and blood hadn't revealed the matter to him (Matthew 16:17). In your flesh, you can say you know who someone is, but it takes a revelation from God to recognize spiritual things. In the flesh, we spout off words that mean nothing. When opposition comes, we flee because we don't understand how God could be with someone and trouble spring up. We say, "I thought you said God was with you."

I stood up in my church and told them what was going to happen in a certain season. The Lord showed me the spirit of Sheba coming in our church and tearing it up. I stood up and declared what would happen concerning the spirit of Sheba. Sheba came into the church and took some sheep out with her. Do you know why? Because people have ears and they can't hear. Just because you have ears on the sides of your head doesn't mean you have ears to hear what the Spirit is saying. You have to have ears to hear. You have folks without license who are just going out on their own without being able to hear.

This is why I'm finding out that the enemy wants to keep his foot on us. Some of us don't take any junk. I know we have brothers who don't take junk, but there are some sisters who don't take any junk. You can't just shut them up. You can't just get over on them. I'm here to tell you that if you are going to obey God in this hour, it is going to cost you everything. If you're not ready to give up everything, sit down. Turn your license in. Stop asking for open doors. Don't even get up to testify. Sit down if you're not ready to go through the hell and hot water. If you're not ready for people to talk about you, and if you're not ready to lose friends and family, sit down. If you're not ready to cry by yourself, you might as well sit down.

These women knew that they could have been stoned for trying Moses. They didn't have a voice. Who did they think they were, coming up in there saying that they would not be denied? Who did they think they were talking to? I guarantee you; one of them was paying attention to the history lesson. One of them knew that God changes His mind with Noah. They probably didn't say it out loud, but I know that when they got together in their huddle, they recalled what God had done before. They knew that if God did it before, He could do it again. They didn't know exactly what God was going to do, but they were determined to find out. What would you do if you weren't afraid? What would you do? I thought about that thing. We face opposition and we're afraid. There's no need to worry about what people are going to say, because they are already saying. Scratch that off the list. There's no need to worry about what you'll lose because you've lost everything already. Scratch that off the list. What would you do if you weren't afraid? You are the one who cripples you. It's not what someone else is saying; it's what you are saying. It's what you are thinking. It's what you are telling yourself when you lay in the bed at night in the dark. It's what you say when you are alone with God and your thoughts. What are you saying to yourself about what God promised you? What are you saying? We are talking ourselves out of our destiny. We're talking ourselves out of the promises of God. If we were to sit back and look at the status quo, we know that the Southern Baptists have this area hemmed up. Apostolic houses catch hell and get thrown in the midst of a fight because we come to dismantle every mindset and we come to declare the King and His kingdom. When we do that, they come back with their chains and want to know who told us women that we could preach and pastor. They come back to tell us that our position is meant for a man. They know so much that they are missing God. I will not be denied.

Somebody said to me, "Well what are you going to do if you stand before the Lord and He says that He really didn't call women to pastor?" I'm gonna say, "Well, God, here are the souls. I did it because I loved You, Lord. I went out and did what the Word of God told me to do." I will not be denied. You have to stop letting strongholds define you. You're going to have to get in the Word of God and let the Word be your reality. There are so many things in this world that are fighting against what God says you are. You can go into some of these churches and they are bashing this one and bashing that one. Ain't nobody got time for that. Let's just do the will of God. Can we just preach the Gospel of Jesus Christ? Can we just set the captives free? Can we just see the bruised be healed? Nobody knows what it's like to be a woman who's a single parent but a woman who's a single parent. Sometimes you will have to make choices that hurt, and you will look like a plum fool to everybody else. They will question why you did it, they will question who told you to do it, and they will say that God isn't with you.

If God changed the Law for them, what would He do for us if we just had the boldness to go before Him? What would you do if you weren't afraid? Where would you go if you weren't afraid? Who would you be if you weren't afraid? Let me give you a little bit of sociology. So many times we get stuck in stereotypes. We think that because we are women, we are supposed to stay in the house and have 3.2 children and cook and clean. I don't have a problem with that, but guess what? My babies are grown. What's next? You're not getting ready to define me. The Word defines me. I will not be denied. What God said I can do, I'm going to do it. I don't care if you get mad. I don't care if you talk about me. God bless. We are going to do what God says to do.

You have to understand that it is God who orchestrated this opposition. He is the one who turned people against you. He is the one who told them to get up and go. He is the one who told them to leave now. He is the one who told them to talk about you on Facebook. He is the one who told them to hold back their tithes and offerings. He told the ones you poured into and brought out of goofyland to go start a church somewhere and call someone they have never heard of to cover them. What do you do? Sssshhhhh. Say absolutely nothing. Why? Because we legislate on our knees. I can do more on my knees than I can running my mouth to somebody else. It doesn't matter where they go. The only thing that matters is that you do what God tells you to do.

I've found out that fruit has a voice. When Peter denied Jesus, he sat in the circle with them around the fire and they knew by his voice that they had been with Jesus (John 18:15-27). His speech betrayed him. You can get up and go sit under whomever you want to sit under, but when you get up and speak, they are going to hear whom you walked with. Fruit doesn't lie. Fruit has a voice. I will not be denied. They can try to make a fool out of me if they want to - I still won't be denied. Like I said, I will do like those women and stand on the edge of my promise. Better is coming. Greater is coming. God is not unjust to forget our labor of love, and whatever He spoke, He will make it good. If He has to change the Law for you to get what you have to get, He will change the Law. He understands that my reproach is His reproach, so if I look bad, He looks bad. He's not about to look bad in front of anybody. Fruit doesn't lie. It has a voice.

We have to learn to let God fight our battles. I don't do this public fighting stuff. I don't care what anybody else is saying. I don't want anybody from my church getting involved in any public brawls. The Bible says that the way is even spoken of because of us (2 Peter 2:2). I want to get myself out of that equation. I have enough stuff going on with me. I don't have time to miss out on my inheritance. I don't have time to fight with anybody because it's not about them. It's a distraction. I've never seen so much distraction in all my life. There's so much stuff going on at the left and the right that you can't concentrate. I understand that the Scripture tells me that the enemy will come to wear out the patience of the saints (Daniel 7:25). The enemy comes and tries to grind you to powder. He tries to make you give up on God. He tries to make you give up on your promise. He tries to make you throw in the towel. What you're going to have to do is get back in the presence of God and remind Him of what He said. God told us to put Him in remembrance of what He has said (Isaiah 43:26). It isn't because He forgot - He wants to make sure that you didn't forget. Some of us are absent-minded, especially when we start going through.

The Lord spoke to me and said that these daughters of Zelophehad were a prophetic preshadowing of what it was going to take in these last days to enter into the promises of God. We are first going to have to stand against tradition. We are going to have to stand against the traditions of men and against what our aunts and grandmothers have said. God needs us to break the mold because what He wants to do in you, you have never seen it before. What God wants to say to you is something you have never heard before. What God wants to manifest through you is something He has never done before. You are going to have to break the mold in order to be what God said for you to be.

The next thing you are going to have to do is stand against those old paradigms. You will have to stand against those old things that are locked in especially in our area (the Carolinas). We know that there are principalities and powers that we are standing against. I never knew that there was such a fight against women. I was totally oblivious. I was just shouting and praising God with no idea that this fight even existed. All kinds of stuff started happening, and I had to figure out what was going on. It was like I got hit with a curve ball. God said to me, "This that you are experiencing is a stronghold in your area. This is a stronghold in the region, and I have set women in position in that region because that principality wants to stand against what I have decreed. I need someone who is willing to be bold. I need someone who is willing to risk it all and lay down their life for this gospel. I need someone who doesn't care about what people say and what they may lose. I need someone who doesn't mind looking like a fool in front of everybody else. I need someone who knows how I operate who is willing to be my voice." Can you be God's voice? Can you answer the call? This isn't about walking across the stage and getting your license. That's the easiest part.

The fight begins after the easy part. What if your enemies become them of your own household? What if everything around you looks like you're cursed and not blessed? That's when the fight begins. What do you do when it looks like every door that was about to be opened is closed in your face? What do you do when the battle is in public and not in private? What do you do when everybody in your city has your business on blast? That's when the fight begins. Can you still show your face knowing that they talked about you? Can you still just stick to the Word when they're talking about you? Can you still just walk in humility and thank God anyhow, no matter what's going on? Can you do that? What would you do if you weren't afraid? That's what I would do. I would hold my peace. I would wait on God. I wouldn't try to explain myself. I'd wait until my change comes like Job did. I'd still get outside and preach this Word whether they were here or there. I would still come up and see my sisters and brothers and hug them like nothing happened. And guess what? I'm not scared, so I can do that.

Fear has the ability to cripple you. It won't just cause you to be hindered; it will cripple you. 2 Timothy 1:7 declares: "For God hath not given us the spirit of fear; but of power, and of love, and of a sound

76

mind." The first place the enemy tries to put that fear is in our mind. He will have us thinking people are talking about us who aren't even thinking about us. Then when we get in the presence of people who are really talking about us, we don't even realize that they are really talking about us. We have got to get to the place where we do not allow anything to stand in the way of what God has said. It is going to take a ruthless people to receive the promises of God. I believe that we are sitting on the verge of one of the greatest revivals that we have ever seen and that we ever will see. I believe that the book of Acts doesn't even parallel to what God wants to do through us. This is why God is taking us through this death walk. This is why God is trying our hearts. This is why God is trying to see if we love the world and our families more than we love Him. He wants to see if we love our cars, houses and jobs more than we love Him. He wants to see if we love our children more than we love Him. He wants to know if you love your reputation more than you love Him. If you love all of these things more than Him, then He can use you. If you can lay aside your life, lay down and die, and let God resurrect you in the presence of the same ones you were crucified in front of, then God can use you. If you're not ready to be crucified, you're not ready to be resurrected. If you're not ready to be resurrected, you're not ready to be used. It's going to

77

take death in order for God to use us. Have you ever been to a funeral? You know that when you see that dead person laying there, you can punch them in the face, tell them off, curse them out, and even pour liquor on them - they won't lick their lips and they will not come back to life. They're dead. We're not there yet. When folks talk about us we immediately respond and defend ourselves. We're ready to fight. If they did this to Jesus, then they are going to do this to us. What Bible have you been reading? You'd better put down that children's storybook. They put too much sugar in that and it isn't truth. 2 Timothy 3:12 states, "Yea, and all that will live godly in Christ Jesus shall suffer persecution."

I was talking to one of my spiritual sons and he was talking about a scandal. I told him that this is the hour when God would move in the hearts of those who have been sitting in obscurity. He's moving in the hearts of those He can trust and those who He has tried in the fire. He is moving in those who have no reputation among men, because they have already lost it all. God has already replacing these proud and arrogant people with people who don't care about a name and honorariums and fame. He's raising up people who just want to preach Jesus and Him crucified. People who want to see lives changed. We want to see people healed, delivered, and set free.

Woman, you have to get yourself together if you're going to see this. You have to stop playing with your salvation. Stop letting everybody define you. Stop listening to the voice inside your head unless it lines up with the Word of God. Get on your face. Defy stereotypes. Defy the laws of men. Our God legislates in the heavens. He doesn't just rule, He super-rules. He has watchers who will decree on our behalf as they did in the book of Daniel. In twelve months' time, we will see what has been declared for us. You have to believe your God. The Bible says in Daniel 11:32, "And such as do wickedly against the covenant shall he corrupt by flatteries: but the people that do know their God shall be strong, and do exploits." You can't do anything if you don't know God. It's time to get to know the God of your salvation. You're going to have to know Him personally. I don't care about the tears you've been crying. We've all been crying. Wipe your tears. I told the saints at church one time that I was going through, but when I come into the congregation of the mighty, I'm not coming to weep and sob. I'm coming to rejoice. When I cry, I cry by myself. When I weep, I weep by myself. When I come together with the saints

I remember that where there is unity there is strength. I don't have time to cry in front of you. I'm fighting. I don't have time to be crying. Fight now and cry later.

Once upon a time, we did what we had to do to get what we had to get. Now we are spoiled and we don't know how to fight. We don't want to go to church when the air conditioner is broken. We forget that hell is hotter than it is outside. Why do we act like we were born with air conditioners attached to us? We pick the churches we're going to attend based on how good their air conditioning is. We take too much for granted because we are playing church. We aren't getting it. We change churches like we change socks. When they don't do what we want us to do, we say that we've received all that we can receive from them. What spirit is that? If they make it past that two-year honeymoon, you might be doing good, but then when you hit that fourth year, it becomes a question. We come together to encounter God. You should be able to sit beside your neighbor and feel what they're going through if you have the real Holy Ghost. Instead, we look for the pastor to do everything. We have the same Holy Ghost. This is why our leaders are dying, because we are overdoing stuff. I am not praying for the whole church. If you have some Holy Ghost, come on and help. We have to be bold. We have to be strong. We have to know that just as He told Joshua, the Lord is with us. I don't care what it looks like. I don't care if you're crying. I don't care if they talked about you and if your name is mud. My name is mud as it relates to people. But I know that my name is not mud in the presence of God. They can say what they like. I'm not moved by that. If God says anything different then I'm in trouble. As long as I'm hearing what He's saying, bless the Lord. If He starts saying something else, I may have to sit down. You have to know what God is saying about you.

These women knew something in them. Something within them refused to allow them to settle. Something within them said "We know that these men are going to look at us like we're crazy. We know that they're going to say that we're not entitled to this." The battle was really about the fact that their ancestors were Josephs' children. Their inheritance had just been reinstated. They weren't about to give it up. Do you know how long it was for them to even get anything because they were separated? God brought them together and just because they were girls, they weren't supposed to have it. The devil is a liar. God made them girls and He knew what He was doing. Stop fighting who you are. Let every reality that is not like God fall out. I will not be denied. I will not take "no" for an answer. I will not let what others say define who I am because I will legislate on my knees. I will move in the presence of God until He moves for me and changes the Law for me. I'll move until He touches somebody's heart for me and opens a door for me. I will not be moved, and I will not be denied.

Chapter Four

I am UNSHAKEABLE!

Hebrews 12:27-29 (KJV)

"And this word, Yet once more, signifieth the removing of those things that are shaken, as of things that are made, that those things which cannot be shaken may remain. Wherefore we receiving a kingdom which cannot be moved, let us have grace, whereby we may serve God acceptably with reverence and godly fear: For our God is a consuming fire."

I want to just go back to the twenty-sixth verse, and I want to read to you from the Amplified Bible and then I want to look again at the Message Bible so that you will have a different translation.

Hebrews 12:26-29 (Amplified Bible)

"Then [at Mount Sinai] His voice shook the earth, but now He has given a promise: Yet once more I will shake and make tremble not only the earth but also the [starry] heavens. Now this expression, Yet once more, indicates the final removal and transformation of all [that can be] shaken—that is, of that which has been created—in order that what cannot be shaken may remain and continue. Let us therefore, receiving a kingdom that is firm and stable and cannot be shaken, offer to God pleasing service and acceptable worship, with modesty and pious care and godly fear and awe; For our God [is indeed] a consuming fire."

Hebrews 12:26-29 (The Message)

"His voice that time shook the earth to its foundations; this time—he's told us this quite plainly—he'll also rock the heavens: "One last shaking, from top to bottom, stem to stern." The phrase "one last shaking" means a thorough housecleaning, getting rid of all the historical and religious junk so that the unshakable essentials stand clear and uncluttered.

Do you see what we've got? An unshakable kingdom! And do you see how thankful we must be? Not only thankful, but brimming with worship, deeply reverent before God. For God is not an indifferent bystander. He's actively cleaning house, torching all that needs to burn, and he won't quit until it's all cleansed. God himself is Fire!"

I Corinthians 15:57-58 (KJV)"

"But thanks be to God, which giveth us the victory through our Lord Jesus Christ. Therefore, my beloved brethren, be ye steadfast, unmovable, always abounding in the work of the Lord, forasmuch as ye know that your labour is not in vain in the Lord."

Acts 20:22-24 (KJV)

"And now, behold, I go bound in the spirit unto Jerusalem, not knowing the things that shall befall me there: Save that the Holy Ghost witnesseth in every city, saying that bonds and afflictions abide me. But none of these things move me, neither count I my life dear unto myself, so that I might finish my course with joy, and the ministry, which I have received of the Lord Jesus, to testify the Gospel of the grace of God."

I want to encourage you because I know that we have been going through changes, situations, circumstances and difficulties. I need you to prophesy to yourself because the word you prophesy to yourself will change your life. I need you to profess over your life: "I will not be shaken. You know why? Because I'm unshakable."

The Bible tells us that there is a shaking that was coming and the things that were shaken had to be shaken so that those things that could not be shaken could remain. I know sometimes we tend to

85

mourn and grieve when we suffer losses, but you have to understand that even as we read in these verses, we are from an unshakable kingdom. Even though my life might be shaken and even though everything around me is shaken, I will not be moved. This is the time of some of the weakest wimpiest people who call themselves believers. So many people have no backbone and can't go through anything. They are always snotting, crying and breaking down. Now listen, I snot and cry too, but you best believe that I snot and cry in private. When I am out here on the battlefield, I don't have time for any tears. Anybody who has ever been in the service will tell you that there is no time to be worried about how you feel and how much you want to be at home instead of out there on the front line. You have an enemy you are facing and you don't have any time to worry about what's going on. The only thing you can think about is "If that enemy shows up I'm gonna blow his head off." What happens with us is that we get distracted by life's happenings. We get distracted by who doesn't like us and by who's talking about us. We get distracted about how many friends we have today and how many friends walked away from us. We think about whether or not our church is going and who is going to stay or walk away. We get distracted about whether or not we will have enough money to pay our bills. Listen. If I don't have enough,

I'm still unshakable. When all hell is breaking loose, you have to understand what you are made of, where you come from and what you've been born out of. You are not just your mother's child. You have been begotten of God. What happens is that you don't know what your spiritual DNA is and because you haven't connected the dots, you still think you're just "so-and-so's child" and that your older brother is a crybaby and you oldest sister is a wimp too, and they don't know how to go through anything. So whenever you start going through your tests and your fire, you start acting like your brothers and sisters. I'm here to tell you that I don't have time for wimpy kids.

We come to church and we want to be soft. "Can't you just love me? Can't you just give me a hug?" Yes, I will hug you, love you and tell you to go on back out there. We go through tests and we go through trials, but how many can say like Paul said in the book of Acts, "But none of these things move me." Even though we may not want to have to deal with what we are going through, we have to have that confession in our trial. We might talk tall, but when those situations come we get moved. You are going to have a thick skin if you're going to live with God in these last days. You have to be able to take something. You've got to be able to get with somebody who can see further than you can see. Some of us have vision problems. We have to get with someone who has 20/20 vision in the Spirit. When you have 20/20 vision in the Spirit you can look beyond what you're going through. I understand that your marriage may be on the rocks. I understand that your kids may be acting up. I understand that you may not have all the money that you desire. You can't pay your bills on time. I understand you have high blood pressure, anxiety, diabetes, and you're believing God for a healing. I understand that - but when are you going to get the mentality that you're unshakable and that no matter what, you will not let any of these things move you?

We have to get to the place where we are unshakable in our prayer life and in our standing on the Word of God. If someone comes in your house and messes with your stuff, you will be ready to fight. We want to get the guns and go after folks - and we are church folks, saved, sanctified and filled with the Holy Ghost. But what do we do in spiritual things? Why is it that we seem to just fall down and cry and get up under the bench and just let whatever happens happen? What happened to your fight? What happened to your drive? What happens to your "Whatever it takes God, I'm gonna live for you"? Where is that? All the things we see going on in the news today, the enemy is on a rampage. Why aren't we on a rampage in the Spirit? Why isn't the church sounding off about all the hell that's breaking loose? We should be talking louder than the psychics and so-called gurus. Instead, all we hear is a whisper from the church. Why? Because we're jelly backs. We can't' take anything. We're looking at the Word but we're not eating this Word. We aren't digesting the fact that we really are supposed to be an unshakable people. Guess what? We haven't even seen all that we will see. If you can't go through this little Mickey Mouse test, how are you talking about you want to get out here and be somebody's apostle or pastor? We want titles. I have never seen so many title holding people in all my days. Call me Sister Boo Boo, my name is Fran. The only thing that matters to me is that when I open my mouth God shows up. That's the only thing I care about. I want to be able to get a prayer through. I want to know that God moves at the sound of my voice. That's the only thing that matters. Instead, we get caught up in pomp and circumstance and what people think. We worry about looking good and smelling good and sounding good (now please make sure you look good and smell good). It's not about the outward appearance. You have people who have the complete package but they can't take anything. We're seen that even in our ministry: folks who talk in tongues and brag and boast, but as soon as the hellhounds break

89

out, they are gone. Do you understand what it takes for you to stand on the front line? I'm not talking about being on the sideline. I said front line. Do you understand that your very life is at stake? Do you understand that you have to have a mentality that says you won't flinch, and that whatever it takes you will do what God has called you to do? That when you leave this earth you need to be able to say that you have accomplished everything that God has commanded you to do? It's not about a shout. I like to shout whenever I can, but it's not about that. It's about seeking His face and going after Him.

This is a sidebar... The Pharisees were upset because the disciples were out in the field eating. They asked Jesus why His disciples didn't fast and He said, ""How can the guests of the bridegroom mourn while he is with them? The time will come when the bridegroom will be taken from them; then they will fast." (Matthew 9:15, NIV)

Here's the problem: When you mourn for someone, your heart cries for them. What Jesus was saying is that when is not here we should have a mourning in our spirit for Him. We don't mourn for the bridegroom because we have our programs, our money in the bank, we can get our hair done, and we can get our nails done and buy shoes... We are not mourning for Him. When we get back to mourning for the bridegroom we will see the bridegroom show up. This is why the Word can be preached and people will just sit there staring. If we were at a game, it would be standing room only and I would not even be able to hear the person sitting next to me. We don't eat the Word. We watch television for hours upon hours upon hours. We cannot be unshakable watching R-rated movies. How are you going to be saved and you're watching people having sex on television? This is why we fall into the first thing that comes. I'm not talking about people who just got saved. I'm talking about leaders. We don't have any "stick to it". Where is our conviction? Don't we understand that the enemy is lulling us to sleep? You can't preach against what you indulge in. If my mindset is "bang bang, shoot 'em up" I can't get mad if they start shooting in my neighborhood. I like watching it on TV so how can I get mad about them doing it in my neighborhood? How can I go into the spirit of bondage that I indulge in? We are from an unshakable kingdom and we need to have an unshakable mentality. In order to get that, we have to serve an unshakable God. We have to pray. We have to read the Word. We have to fast.

Everything that can be shaken will be shaken. Prophetically speaking, 2012 was a rough year - it was a doozie. But when 2011 was here, we danced, we shouted, and were excited about going into 2012. But then when God took the belt out and started to bring order and structure trying to align us, we started running from Him. So there we sat, on the edge of 2013, Even though, spiritually, we were already in 2013: Coming out of a rough time, because we had to get our butts whooped for twelve months. I don't think I have ever cried so much as I cried in 2012. Even though I cried, my heart resolved that none of those things would move me. God has a purpose for all the things that we have been enduring. He wants to show us what He really created us for. We think we're created for one thing but God has a way of showing us what He really created us for. Some things He has to make plain for us. We don't always speak English too well and we need a little sign language because we miss it. We have come through a whole season of nothing but going through and all we had was a promise. We didn't see anything manifest. We saw everything blow up. I had to keep preaching with a straight face like nothing had happened. The phone was still ringing. People still needed prayer and counseling. I couldn't take it out on the saints and be nasty and bash them over the pulpit when I was going through. We were all going through. Now that we have gotten ourselves in alignment, and now that we understand what it was all about, none of these things will move us. You had to do through that shaking so that you could see what you would be left with. Truth be told, we are not left with what we thought we would be left with. I have had some of my most staunch supporters who would always say, "Whatever you need, I'm there" - where are they? Everybody has not been created to go all the way to the end with you. Everybody has not been created for that. Everybody who said, "Oh I love you! I love you!" - where are they? The moment you talk the godly belt out and try to bring correction, their story changes. If you are so anointed that you can't get correction, sit down because you're not ready.

Let me give you another sidebar. The anointing flows down. There is no such thing as a self-made man. All of these people running around here with all of these titles saying that the Lord said that they were apostles and chief apostles but they don't have a church and nobody knows where they came from. The anointing flows downward. God is about a corporate move. His house is about a corporate anointing. The anointing flows down just like it flowed down to Aaron's beard and onto his garment (Psalm 133:2), and then we will

93

receive the anointing. We are coming back to a season of us sitting at the feet of men and women of God. God is going to allow all of this stuff to shake around us so that we can see what we have and what we don't have. I went through hell in my own house. I told my armor bearers not to come in the house but to stay outside. I told them to pull up in the yard and beep the horn and I would come outside. All the while, I was on my face reminding God of what He said. Can you still keep preaching when all hell breaks loose? When things around you start falling down, will you still serve God? This is the hour for us to see what we're really made of. I'm not talking about us being made of "sugar and spice and everything nice" because that's malarkey. This testing fire is going to show us what we're made of. Some of us can't even take eighty-degree weather - let's not talk about the fire of God. We say that we want to shine for Jesus. We were singing a song, "This Little Light of Mine" and I love that song, but here's the problem: You can't shine until you're first burned. Ain't no shining until you burn. You haven't even gotten in the fire yet and you're talking about you're shining. You're not shining. Sit down. All of this nonsense and tomfoolery that we say is God is not God. We can't sit up under a strong word because we get mad and offended and we walk away. We act like people don't like us. I had someone tell me that they don't

EVER miss it. I told them, "Well you missed it this time love. Deuces." Your pride will go before your fall. God is not enlisting proud folks. If you can't sit under your leaders, you don't need to lead. We have to go back to the place where we honor those who lead us and pray for us and fast for us and cry out to God for us. I was talking to a person on the phone and I had to ask them, "Who is your overseer? Why are you mad because your overseer didn't send you any money? Do you have a job?" He said he was in full-time ministry. He only had two members. I told him to get a full-time job. Who sent you? Where did you come from? What Cracker Jack box did you get your license from, because clearly nobody with some good sense sent you? He said his overseer was anointed. He said he didn't like gifted people he needed anointed people. I told him that gifted and anointed was the same thing. I told him that his impartation didn't come from a man's anointing but from a man's character. Who he or she is, that's from where they pour. Someone can be anointed and still be dirty and you're drinking from that cup. It's not about our anointing. It's about our character. We have to let God deal with the real us - the one we don't let church folks see. We are still unshakable. This is why we have to shake all of that other nonsense off. How are we going to be used of God if we have no hunger for the things of God? This is what the shaking is about. God has to let us see how religious we have become. We have the shout down to a science, we can speak in tongues, but we are nutty and religious. We have to get beyond the shake and the noise and get some substance on the inside. When somebody comes into your presence what do you have to offer them? What are you pouring out of you? The last TV show you watched? We can sit down and watch a two-and-a-half to three-hour movie. We will be intently watching every minute. We will watch people having sex on TV for hours but on Sunday we want to shout and lay hands. I'm gonna need for you to keep your hands to yourself. I don't want an impartation of Scandal. I need somebody that's in the presence of God. If you've been in His presence then we can talk. But if you haven't been in His presence I need you to keep Scandal and all that other stuff to yourself. Keep that. I will have to go in by myself until God tells me what I need. I'm trying to be unshakable and you're trying to shake me down! Loose here!

We have to be a people who know how to stand a test. We've got to be able to endure hardness as good soldiers (II Timothy 2:3). Do you know that we are going to have to be able to endure the things that are coming before we get out of here? According to some people's theology we shouldn't even be here right now. What manner of people are we to be (II Peter 3:11)? They have a program out about the sisterhood. It's about first ladies, and it's the most abominable foolishness I have ever seen. If this is who is leading the church, this is why we are in trouble. First of all, they're on TV half naked and drinking wine. Let's talk about this wine-drinking spirit. Everybody wants a bottle of Moscato. Get delivered. God still delivers from alcohol. It's ridiculous. They have these women on TV and I told the pastor who sent me the link that I was appalled. I didn't want to watch that mess. That is not who I am. This is not a good representation of the people of God. They were sitting there with catfights and nonsense's and putting it on TV to make the world think that the church is full of a bunch of buffoons. This is why I say we have to sound off. The world is already making an assumption about who we are. This is not the time for us sitting back being good Christians and being quiet. We need to open our mouths. The Bible says to "Cry aloud and spare not" (Isaiah 58:1). Hollywood doesn't know what it's like to be saved. How is Hollywood going to interpret holiness? How are we going to let Hollywood interpret what is godly and what's not godly? Are we going to be real leaders that give to a life of consecration and prayer and fasting? This is the season of self-sacrifice. If you're going to get anything from God, you're going to have to sacrifice self. You're going

97

to have to kill self. If you don't want to kill self, you'd better exit stage right while you can. I told the Lord that I didn't want any of those religious folks coming into Sure Word. I don't want saved folks. Give me folks off the street. Do you know why? Because they know where they are and they appreciate truth. Church folks say they love the truth. No. I became your enemy because I told you the truth (Galatians 4:16). Church people boast about telling the truth and telling it like it is but their tune changes when it is time for them to hear the truth and hear someone else tell it like it is to them. It is time for us to be an unshakable people. Unshakeable to the point that we do not relent or give up on what we are trusting God for. We have His Word, and His Word will never change. He said, "Heaven and earth will pass away, but my words will never pass away." (Matthew 24:35) You have to understand that even if everybody who ever promised something to you broke their promise, He will never break His promise. When we get that understanding, we won't allow our circumstances and situations to move us out of God. You won't let whomever walks away from you keep you from doing what God says to do. We keep saying that we'll go if we have to go buy ourselves. Keep singing that song because you're getting ready to have to go by yourself.

One of these days I'll testify and tell the whole story, but if I had to go through the things I had to go through in this season, I know that all hell was breaking loose in a lot of people's lives. Every message I have preached was tested. Everything I ever said to God was tested. You said "for God I live and for God I'll die" and we will see. When your head gets on the chopping block, what are you going to say? Are you going to cry, or are you going to stay there and sacrifice self because you know that none of these things are going to move you? You have to get serious about your walk with God. If ever you have been serious about anything, you have got to be serious about your relationship with God. Friends will walk away from you. Marriages end in divorce sometimes. Churches split up. You have to know that you know that you know that God's Word is settled in heaven (Psalm 119:89). I don't care if this building implodes, explodes or does whatever. We have to know that if we die before time, God must be about to raise us back up. I was trying to tell the church to get their appetite ready for the things of God and for what I feel God pulling us to. I was trying to get them to study the revivals and the healing evangelists because we have come to church and grown accustomed to such foolishness. We call all of this foolishness "God" and we don't even know how to sacrifice. Unless you have an ailment or something going on that prevents you from being outside of the house, most of your going to church is just to see what's going on. We have to get to the place that we'll lay aside every weight AND the sin that does so easily beset us (Hebrews 12:1). If you read that chapter it talks about how we are compassed about with a great cloud of witnesses. Who is Paul talking about? He is talking about the people who have gone on before us. Do you know that they are standing in heaven spurring on? They did their part and they are counting on us to bring the ball home for the team. If you read that chapter, you will see that the Bible says that they cannot receive the promise without us and we can't receive it without them. Do you understand what that means? That means that there is a work that they began that God is counting on us to finish. The Bible says that we all run but one gets the prize (I Corinthians 9:24). The corporate man gets the prize. We, the Body of Christ get the prize, but we have to have the right mindset. We have to get the mindset that we are unshakeable and that we will not be moved. I have had to deal with all kinds of crazy stuff. My son called me and told me that they were about to play vodka pong. I said, "What is that? Are you actually telling me that you're about to get drunk? Are you really telling me that?" I had to push all of that aside. I am unmovable. I am unshakeable. I have one daughter out there doing all kinds of stuff. I have told her a million times, "Turn your body inside out, do whatever you want to do, but you WILL live for the Lord." I have His Word. We have to get to the place that regardless of what's going on, we still prophesy to our circumstances. Don't let your circumstances prophesy to you. Don't let your life tell you what you're going to do and what you're not going to do. You are supposed to tell your life, "This is what we are doing." Unshakable. I will not be moved. I'm not gonna be moved in my prayer life, I'm not gonna be moved in my fasting, I'm not gonna be moved from standing on the Word, I'm not gonna be moved from confessing the Word, I'm not gonna be moved from my place of faith and trust and belief. There is a song that asks, "What do you do when everything around you is shaking and everything around you is moved?" The latter verse says, "I will learn to trust and lean and depend on Jesus." I called my friend on the phone - we like to call people on the phone and get their opinion and get them to pray for us and tell us what the Lord wants us to do. No. Can you get on your face? We are getting ready to see the value of a prayer life. There is value that supersedes dollars and cents. There is value in a prayer life. You have got to be determined that you will do the thing that God has destined you to do. You've got to do it. You must do it. I don't' care what anybody else says. They are going to talk whether you do it or not, so you might as well do it. I know people talk but I don't care. I try to give them something good to say. They talked about Jesus. They lied on Him. They made up stores. Why are we trying to chase stories down? None of these things move me. Stop letting gossip move you. When someone comes to you to gossip, ask them, "Well what did you say?" When someone comes with gossip, they are telling on themselves too. We have to get to the place that we don't let anybody come to us and talk about our man of God and woman of God. How are you going to receive and eat from that table when you have disrespected and dishonored it? You haven't honored it. I say at my church all the time that you cannot receive from who you dishonor. If you dishonor me, you will pay attention to nothing I say. We have to get to place that we look higher than the man and we see Jesus. I don't care how crazy they look, how crazy they sound or how hard the word is. Look for Jesus. Where is God in all that is being said?

Chapter Five

It's Time for Change

I want to talk to those who are not alignment. Those who are dragging their feet and not doing what they are supposed to be doing. At times I can be a prophet, but this is a word from God coming through an apostle. I need for you to be able to understand something: If you are going to be able to do what God has called you to do, you are going to have to get in alignment. That goes for all of us. There's assignment that has to be fulfilled. When you don't fulfill your assignment, hell is your home. Jesus said that the children of the Kingdom would be cast into outer darkness (Matthew 8:12). That means that there are some folks who are naming the name of Jesus who are going to hell. They sing a song in North Carolina that says, "Do you want to go to hell? Hell no!" I'm not cursing, but I don't want to go. That's a song. I'm not saying I want to go to hell and I'm not cursing either. I don't want to go to hell.

Let's look at Romans 12:1 (KJV): "I beseech you therefore, brethren, by the mercies of God, that ye present your bodies a living sacrifice, holy, acceptable unto God, which is your reasonable service."

What God has required of you is reasonable. Let me explain something to you. If you get this now, you can shout later. Before God sends revival He must first send rebuke. Before He sends revival, He must first send a word of judgment. He needs to give you the opportunity to decide who is on the lord's side. God is speaking to us. Paul was saying that he was begging and pleading with the Romans. He put emphasis on his request that they present their bodies as living sacrifices. What does God do with sacrifices? Sacrifices are meant to be killed. You put them on the altar for slaughter. The thing that's wrong with us is that we love our lives too much. We like to live. We like everything that God has to offer. We like all of our perks and our 401k's. I don't have a problem with any of that stuff. The problem is that we don't have those things - those things have us. They have gotten in the way of our pursuit of God. We seek after position and we seek after money. We seek after fame and after all of these carnal things, but we don't seek after God. We don't want to go to prayer before church. We don't have time for that.

You have to understand that you have to position yourself for what God has called you to do. Yes the grace of God is on our lives, and God gives us grace to do what we need to do, but there are some things you are just going to have to put the pedal to the metal on. You are just going to have to put your shoulder to the plow and work. Paul pleads with the Romans and he says to them that he is begging them because of God's mercy that they do something. This was for their benefit. They needed to be holy. For some of us, that is a curse word because we don't know what holiness is any more than we know the man in the moon. We're holy when we come to church. We sing our song and we dance our dance, and that' is okay because the Psalm 100 tells us to make a joyful noise until the Lord. There is something about a people that is intimate with God. There is something about a people that has a relationship with God and spends time with God and God spends time with them. They're not satisfied with the ordinary because they know that there is something more in God and they seek to get it. If you're going to get it, you will have to have a pure heart and clean hands.

There is a wicked thing that calls itself "The Bride of Christ" that does everything but live holy. When you read the book of Revelations it talks about how the bride makes herself ready. This means that there is a preparation that is taking place. What are you preparing yourself for? We prepare ourselves to go to college, we prepare ourselves for job interviews, but are we preparing to meet our God? What kinds of preparations are we making?

You are not able to do what you are supposed to do in the church because you're not doing what you're supposed to do for God. Don't think that what I'm saying is to just come down on you. You can go to YouTube and you will see that this is who I am. God has given me a mandate. We are not going to let anything move us from our assignment. Any time you see hell breaking loose and things trying to take place, it is because God has sanctioned a thing and the enemy is trying to stop the move of God. Why? Because God knows and the enemy knows, if someone hears this Word (that knows God has been dealing with their heart - convicting them of their sinful selves), true repentance will take place. We have to present ourselves to God.

Romans 12:2 says, "And be not conformed to this world: but be ye transformed by the renewing of your mind, that ye may prove what is that good, and acceptable, and perfect, will of God."

It's time for change. It is time for the people of God to change their ways. It is time for us to change from coming up with all these excuses for why we're not doing what we're supposed to do. I have a saying about how we do things for Pharaoh (your boss on your secular job) all the time. We break our necks for Pharaoh. If Pharaoh tells us to make those bricks, we say, "Yes sir, Pharaoh" and we make those bricks. If Pharaoh says that he's taking your straw from you and that you have to figure out another way to make the bricks, you say, "That's okay Mr. Pharaoh, we're gonna make sure we get it done." But when God requires something of us and God's leaders require something of us, why do we half-step? It's time for change.

The real deal is that everybody doesn't want change. God bless our President, and I don't speak any evil about our leaders, but his campaign for the first four years was all about change. The more they tried to change, the more we stayed the same. It's easy to say but it's hard to do. How do I know? Because Jeremiah 13:23 says, "Can the

Ethiopian change his skin, or the leopard his spots? then may ye also do good, that are accustomed to do evil." It's impossible for a leopard to change his spots. We had a saying in the world that "old habits die hard". There are some things that we just don't want to let go of because we like them. The truth of the matter is that we like our mess. We like our foolishness. We like half-stepping. It makes us feel like we aren't responsible for anything. You cannot expect to receive anything if you are not in line. In Revelation 22:12 Jesus said, "And, behold, I come quickly; and my reward is with me, to give every man according as his work shall be." Payday is coming. How much are you going to get paid? Let's look at what you're doing here? Are you following instructions? Can anybody trust you with anything? Can your leaders trust you?

We teach in our School of Prophets that there is a test of obedience. One of the tests of obedience is "Do I ask questions after a command is given?" Another question is: "Can I follow delegation of authority?" We have to follow instructions. We give God lip service and we give leadership lip service. We don't do what we are told because our hearts are not in God. We don't have time to play because folks are busting hell wide open every single day. We have the mindset that we have to hit it and quit it, but we have to understand that there is no excuse for our being lazy. Church is the only place where people jockey for position and when they get it, they do nothing with it. We want to do what looks like will be the thing that gets us accolades. We want to be in charge. We want to be able to say that the pastor wants us to be over a committee, but we can't tell you the last time the committee had a meeting. What's wrong with us? What are we doing? This is not a social club. This is not a social club. This is not the place where you come and pay your dues and get membership. I know the song for the COGIC that says, "You cannot join in, you have to be born in" because I have some COGIC roots - but let me tell you: the Body of Christ is the same way. I don't care about how much you give in your tithes and your offerings. I don't care about how much you come and vacuum the church. If your heart is not in God then you are not in here. It's time for change.

We can't be conformed to the world. The reason why we are disobedient is because we don't have victory in our minds. The reason why I cannot embrace change in the Spirit is because my mind isn't saved. My mind is still a slave to the world's mentality. My mind has not yet been set free and delivered by the power of God. Because of that, I can't follow instruction in the house. Because of that, I can't submit to authority. "Submit" is another curse word in the church. This word "transform" is not just a change of your garments; it's a complete change in figure. It means that everything about you including your form changes. How you do things changes. How you handle situations changes. How you talk changes. How you think changes. If you want to change your behavior, you have to first change your thinking.

I like to go to the root of the matter, so let's talk about why our minds are not saved. We're not delivered and saved in our minds because we have refused to get the Word in our hearts. We don't read our bibles. How am I going to have my mind renewed when I don't pick the Bible up? We don't feel like reading. There is no reason in the world why you can't get some Word in you. You can Google a bible verse. Most of our cell phones have bible apps on them. You can listen to your phone and it will read the Bible to you. The reason you don't eat the Word is because you're not hungry for it. We have to get serious about this thing.

What happened to our brokenness when we come into the presence of the Lord? We want people to shout us to death. We want prophecies and we want everybody to tell us what the Lord said. I'm telling you what the Lord said right now. Why don't we holler and shout over a rebuke? It's still a prophetic word. People have it twisted. Our ears itch for something that is going to encourage us and make us feel good. Today I'm encouraging you to live saved. I'm encouraging you to walk in deliverance and to get for real about your salvation.

There are people who have the propensity and the ability to lead, but they refuse to get into position. The Lord gave me Hebrews 5:12-13 which says, "For though by this time you ought to be teachers, you need someone to teach you again the basic principles of the oracles of God. You need milk, not solid food, for everyone who lives on milk is unskilled in the word of righteousness, since he is a child." (English Standard Version) Why? You are responsible for your own maturity in the Spirit. The church experience is a vitamin and a supplement. It's not the end all, be all. You don't live off this. It's just a shot to get you through until you get another shot. We have gotten to a place of believing that as long as we come to church and hear the Word and get "under the anointing" we're okay. No, you have to get a relationship with the Lord.

I don't have time to tickle people's fancies. People are dying. God has given us assignments in the earth. I want to be able to say, "Lord, I said everything you told me to say. I did everything you told me to do. Yes, somebody might have gotten mad at me, but I did what you told me to do." Because we want to be part of the popularity club, we don't do what God has told us to do. Why? Because we're lazy. It is so much easier for us to stretch out in front of the "hellivision" for four hours than it is to get on our faces and seek God. It's easy for us to do that. It takes work and effort to get into the presence of God. Why is it that we have no longevity? We go after other things more than we go after God. We have people who break their necks to go and be on American Idol and all these other shows, but they have no intimacy with God. None. You spend no time getting any oil in your own lamp, but you want me to pour all of mine out on you? That ain't happening. I'll give you some for your forehead, but you'll have to get the rest yourself. That's what Jesus was talking about when He talked about the ten virgins in Matthew 25. Get your own oil. You have the ability to do so. This ain't the Catholic Church. You aren't coming to church

112

and getting in a booth and having someone to tell you to say twelve Hail Mary's and four Our Fathers in order to be forgiven. The devil is a liar. When God has delivered you from something, you ought to act like you've been delivered. Jesus says in Luke 7:47 that when you are forgiven much you love much. The reason that some of our love has waxed cold is because we have forgotten what we have been forgiven us. We've gotten comfortable in the church. We've gotten to the place where we just come in and want people to sing four songs and shout us for a little bit. We don't remember the mess we did out in the streets.

I was telling the church about how when I was fourteen I went and got a fake id so that I could get drunk. I wanted to get in that liquor store and get some long island iced tea, some gin, and some vodka. I wanted all of that stuff. I come from a family of alcoholics. My family used to do dumb stuff like "let's see if she can hold this liquor". They gave me everything. When I was fourteen I went and got that id. It said that my name was Christine Jackson and that I was twenty-three years. I used that some id to go to the abortion clinic and put my feet in the stirrups and let them snatch a baby out of my womb. When I remember what I was... that's enough for me to run up to the altar. When I think about the fact that I could have died on that table and nobody knew where I was... My family didn't even know I was there. When I think about what God has done for me, how can I let my love run out on Him? How can I play the harlot on God when He has been so good to me? How can I do that when I remember all the men I slept with? I was looking for someone to love me and I didn't understand that sex didn't automatically equal love. When I remember when I met Jesus and when God wrapped His arms around me and fathered me and healed all of my wounds, I don't have a choice but to love Him. How can I not love a God like that? How could I come to church and act like God owes me. How can I come to God's house and the place of worship and refuse to give Him my worship? How can I tell God that I'm gonna do what I want anyway? I can't do that.

I shared with the saints that we have become like Israel. It wasn't so much that Israel sinned against God, but in Israel's sin, Israel began to war against God. They fought God. They decided that they wanted to do what the heathen were doing. They decided that they didn't even want God to be King over them - they asked God to give them a king in the flesh (1 Samuel 8:6). They wanted someone they could lay their eyes on because they felt like God was too far away. We do the same thing. We go running after different preachers. This foolishness they are calling the gospel is not the Gospel at all. Jude 1:3 tells me that I am supposed to "earnestly contend for the faith which was once delivered unto the saints." Contend means to fight. We must fight for the faith that was once delivered to the saints. This watered down pattern that they're serving is ridiculous. You can't even get these people to pray for you. You definitely can't call their phones at 2:00 in the morning for prayer. They will send you to their assistant. What kind of tomfoolery is that? You are a servant. Nobody cares about your title and what you call yourself. I don't care if you wrap your neck up in collars four times over. It doesn't matter. You are a servant. Jesus is coming back for a church without spot, wrinkle or blemish (Ephesians 5:26-27) or any such thing. He's not coming back for this glorified thing we call a church. He's not coming back for this thing that's out here whoring around. That's why He has to get us in order. That's why He has to line us up. That's why He has to rebuke us and whip our behinds until we get in line.

One of the things that aggravate pastoral leadership the most is when folks constantly need a baby bottle and a pacifier. They constantly need for somebody to burp them and diaper them when they should be at this point teaching and burping and diapering others. You should be old enough to be married and have babies but you want to be a baby. We don't want to grow up because it's too much responsibility. We would much rather be Facebook prophets and Facebook apostles and have people follow us online when we aren't living a nickel's worth of dog meat at home. What is your reputation?

Can you just ramble off the vision of the church you attend without looking at a paper? Do you have to look at a piece of paper in order for you to be able to say why you are there? Here's a newsflash: You should be eating and drinking that vision. You should know it backwards and forward, and you should be teaching others the vision of the house just like you teach them the Word, because the vision comes from the Word. Ain't nobody trying to build a kingdom of themselves here. If you don't even know why you are in the ministry you are in, you might want to go back through New Members' Class. Ain't nobody mad but the devil. Ain't nobody God but God.

I'm going to talk to you about this change for a minute. Change means "to become different" and "to make the form, nature, content and future course different from what it was before". When you are changed, your very future and destiny is changed. The destination that you were on your way to gets rerouted because of change that takes place in your life - if you let it.

I'm a Word person, and I like to be able to give you the Word. My opinion is worthless. It might help you and encourage you, but my opinion is not going to deliver you.

Let's look at Micah 7:15-17 (KJV):

"According to the days of thy coming out of the land of Egypt will I shew unto him marvellous things. The nations shall see and be confounded at all their might: they shall lay their hand upon their mouth, their ears shall be deaf. They shall lick the dust like a serpent, they shall move out of their holes like worms of the earth: they shall be afraid of the Lord our God, and shall fear because of thee."

Because of you... This is what we are supposed to look like. Who's afraid of you? I'm not talking about in the sense that you're going to go out in the street and fight. I'm talking about in the sense that they are afraid of what you're packing in the Spirit. Who's afraid of you getting on your knees and praying? Who's afraid of you opening up your mouth and declaring what thus saith the Lord? Who's afraid of you speaking what God says and watching it come to pass? Who's afraid of you? We should cause others to fear the Lord because of the life that we live and the intimacy we have with our Savior. It takes time to cultivate power like that. You don't get it by saying a quick prayer. You are going to have to persevere. Do you know what that means? It means that there has to be a press in your spirit for the things of God. There has to be a hunger and a thirst and a drive for more than what you are. But if you're satisfied with you and with being the status quo, you won't have that perseverance. There's no such thing as an ordinary Christian. When I read my Bible and I see what the Christians did, I realize that these are they who have turned the world upside down. What are you turning upside down? You can't even cast out a headache. You can't put the fear of the Lord in anybody. It is time for change. This weak stuff we are calling church needs to be brought back to the drawing board. We need to lay on our faces before God and hear what He is saying. We need to lay in His presence and get the pattern from Him.

I don't know about you, but I don't want God replacing me. He can replace me. He doesn't have to use me to do anything. Some of us think we're irreplaceable. You go ahead with that mindset, and you just watch. God is able. The Bible says in Psalm 75:6 that He takes down one and puts up another, and He will do it if we don't position ourselves and get in alignment. We need to spend time laying on the altar in prayer. Prayer should be a sacrifice. You should make the sacrifice to be intimate with God. We need to lie on our faces before God and just let Him redo everything about us. We need to get rid of our stinking thinking and begin to offer ourselves before God. We need to allow Him to transform our very lives and make us the vessels that He has ordained for us to be. We haven't even tapped in. Even the prophetic words that have been spoken over us haven't been tapped into yet. We're still peeling back the layers and trying to discover what it is that God is saying. If you don't spend the time with God, you'll never see the fullness of it.

I'm of the persuasion that I have got to pour my life out. I have to. I don't care if it takes all the life out of me. I lived hard in sin, and I'm not coming to God and giving Him less. I'm loud for God like I was loud in the world. I fought in a heartbeat in the world if you touched my stuff - and if you mess with my stuff I will turn my plate down, I will fast and pray and I will send the decrees of the Lord to get my stuff back. You have to get serious. Some people try to talk about how cute I am, but don't let the smooth taste fool you. I love that, because it sets people up to wonder what I'm going to say. Some people look for me to get up there with a weak and soft voice, but I don't have time for that. We have some demons we have to bust. We have lives that need to be transformed. We have people who need to set free. Ain't nobody got time to be cute. I'll throw my hair back and keep right on praying. I'll sweat it all out. I love my shoes, but I'll kick them off in a heartbeat. Don't say it's prayer time, because I'm going IN! That's like ringing the dinner bell for me. I'll meet you there and I'll beat you there.

We have to understand that is our prayers that will birth this end time movement that God is going to send. This is why we must get in prayer. We have to saturate ourselves with prayer. I dare you to turn your plate down and fast. Get hungry for God. Don't come to church looking for the same old same old. We need to look for healing and deliverance and for souls to be set free. We need to look for God to bring us back to our first love. That's what we need to look for. We need to ask God to bring us back to a place of brokenness. We need to ask God to bring us back to a place where we will weep between the porch and the altar. We need to do like the book of Isaiah speaks of and howl for the calamity that has come upon us. We need to do what the Word of God commands us to do. There is serious business. When you got saved, you did not join a week army. You didn't join a cheesy outfit. This is a place where only the strong survive. This is a place where we make the difference between the men and the boys. There is no gender in the Spirit, so I speak to your inner man and I tell you to get in place. Be who God told you to be. Why are you apologizing? I'm really not sorry.

God has set up a time to change us and deliver us. He wants to put His fear in us again. I like to read about the great awakenings and things like that. I was reading one time about how Smith Wigglesworth was sitting on a bench and he never opened his mouth, and there was a man sitting next to him whose heart became convicted because of his sin. Guess what? That came from Wigglesworth's life being smeared in prayer. That came from him being intimate with God. That came from him spending time with the presence of the Lord. It is something when you don't even have to open your mouth and the fear of God precedes you. We need to become a people who are carriers of His anointing. It doesn't just need to be form and fashion. It doesn't just need to be something we talk about. It needs to be something we possess. I'm sick of people talking about it. It's time to be about it. The only way we're going to be about it is that we are going to have to get on our faces. We can all attest that we don't pray like we used to. Time stealers that come to steal our time have robbed us. We set aside time and then something gets in the way of that. We wake up to the alarm but then we snooze and snooze and snooze for another hour and miss our appointment with God.

There is nothing worse than to sit outside and wait for a bus or a train and then miss it. It messes up everything in your day, especially if you have to be somewhere at a certain time. We have to get more about our Father's business. Let's lay aside some of this other stuff. Let's not be religious. Let's really get serious and go after God so that we might apprehend Him for what He has apprehended us for. We need to know why God saved us and why He delivered us. I have to lay my hands on God like He laid His hands on me, and it is possible.

Chapter Six

Overcomer's Image

We are going to talk about the image of an overcomer. What should you look like? What should you sound like? Overcomers don't walk around with their heads hung down. They don't walk around looking sad. Why? Because there is an image we have as overcomers.

Let's look at Genesis 1:11 (King James Version).

"And God said, Let the earth bring forth grass, the herb yielding seed, and the fruit tree yielding fruit after his kind, whose seed is in itself, upon the earth: and it was so."

Genesis 1:27-31 states:

"So God created man in his own image, in the image of God created he him; male and female created he them. And God blessed them, and God said unto them, Be fruitful, and multiply, and replenish the earth, and subdue it: and have dominion over the fish of the sea, and over the fowl of the air, and over every living thing that moveth upon the earth.

And God said, Behold, I have given you every herb bearing seed, which is upon the face of all the earth, and every tree, in the which is the fruit of a tree yielding seed; to you it shall be for meat. And to every beast of the earth, and to every fowl of the air, and to every thing that creepeth upon the earth, wherein there is life, I have given every green herb for meat: and it was so. And God saw every thing that he had made, and, behold, it was very good. And the evening and the morning were the sixth day."

Genesis 5:1-3

"This is the book of the generations of Adam. In the day that God created man, in the likeness of God made he him; Male and female created he them; and blessed them, and called their name Adam, in the day when they were created. And Adam lived an hundred and thirty years, and begat a son in his own likeness, and after his image; and called his name Seth:"

We are image bearers. We bear God's image. He created us to bear His image. There is a phrase used in the Latin, *Imago Dei*, which means "The image of God". Here it is that God has created us to be those who bear His image and His likeness. There is a difference between "likeness" and "image" and we need to learn that difference. Your image is what people see. Your likeness is what reproduces after you. Likeness includes behavior and characteristics. It's those things that make you uniquely you. The Bible tells us that God created man and woman in His image. There are certain things that we should be bearing. There are certain things that we should be carrying and bringing forth in the earth because this is what God created us to do.

We are copies and replicas. We have been handcrafted by God to reflect His image in the earth. Now here's the deal: There are rules and regulations that have to be followed for you to be completely His. We have to be able to follow His prescribed direction and directive like following a recipe. If the recipe calls for two eggs and I put one egg in, I'm going to mess up the recipe. Whatever I'm making is not going to taste right, and it won't have the right consistency. It might look like it, but when I put it in my mouth it won't taste right. This is what I'm talking about when I say "image and likeness". We can look like something but it doesn't mean that we have that something.

Let's look at Revelation 2:7 which says, "He that hath an ear, let him hear what the Spirit saith unto the churches; To him that overcometh will I give to eat of the tree of life, which is in the midst of the paradise of God." This is why you have to be able to understand what your image is. The image that we have is that of an overcomer. Not a victim. We are not victims. Some of us play the victim every time we go through something. We have to lose that mentality. That's a victim mentality and not an overcomer mentality. That is not the image that God created. If I am carrying His image, I have to think like Him. That's Bible. How can I walk in dominion, authority and power if I don't think like God? If I'm thinking like a created man, there will be inhibitions to me being able to fulfill the call of God because my thought process is finite and not infinite. I have to be able to tap into the Spirit so that I can hear God. I have to tap in so that I can understand what it is to walk in the power of God and bear His image. I can't heal the sick and raise the dead until I understand His image. I can't set the captives free until I understand His image. We always ask the question "What would Jesus do?" - That's a dumb question. Pick up your Bible if you don't know what Jesus would do. Nobody should have to ask that question because we should be doing what Jesus would do. That's why we came up with that dumb question, because folks haven't been doing what Jesus would do.

Revelation 2:17 says, "He that hath an ear, let him hear what the Spirit saith unto the churches; To him that overcometh will I give to eat of the hidden manna, and will give him a white stone, and in the stone a new name written, which no man knoweth saving he that receiveth it." Hearing is an active activity. There is an implied behavior that should follow, which means that you are going to do what you hear. He that has an ear, can you use your ears, please, and hear what the Spirit is saying unto the churches? Here it is again: "To him that overcometh will I give to eat of the hidden manna." There are some things that you have to dig out. Isaiah 61:3 talks about how God will give us beauty for ashes. Isaiah 45:3 says, "And I will give thee the treasures of darkness, and hidden riches of secret places, that thou mayest know that I, the LORD, which call thee by thy name, am the God of Israel." You don't get those treasures until you start digging. You don't get those treasures until you have to experience darkness. Have you ever been unhappy before? It changes your perspective. You learn something about your walk with God when you go through. IF you have an ear to hear what the Spirit is saying. But if you do not have an ear to hear, you will go through your situation murmuring and complaining, and your perspective will not change. We think ourselves out of what God is saying. We need to have an ear to hear what God is

127

saying. There are some secret things that God wants to be able to reveal to us, but we are going to have to get in position and understand that He wants to give us those revelations. For some of us, we know that God wants to reveal things to us, but we won't sit still long enough for Him to do it. We won't sit still long enough to hear from God and to allow Him to download in our spirits what we need to receive. There is too much movement in our feet. We are always on the go. I am guilty, but I understand that there are times that I have to sit still in order to be able to hear from God. There are things that God wants to do in us. I cannot be an image bearer of God if I'm constantly walking in flesh.

Let's look at Revelation 3:21- "To him that overcometh will I grant to sit with me in my throne, even as I also overcame, and am set down with my Father in his throne." Overcoming is not just what takes place when you get to heaven. God wants you to understand that the place for you to overcome now is now. When you go to Genesis 1:28, you see that God created male and female with an intended purpose. Their purpose was to be fruitful and multiply, to replenish the earth, and to subdue and have dominion. You can't dominate anything that has dominated you. You have to be able to walk in dominion. You have to think like God. I don't want to think like a man. I don't want to think like Fran, either. I want and need to think like God. My breakthrough is in me thinking like God. My breakthrough is found in Philippians 2:5-6 which tells us to "Let this mind be in you, which was also in Christ Jesus: Who, being in the form of God, thought it not robbery to be equal with God". Say what? Is that what I'm supposed to be thinking? Yes, because I am an heir and a joint-heir with Jesus Christ. What's His is mine. His authority is my authority. His will is my will. It's not what I want to do. What He wants to do is what I want to do. Let this mind be in you. This is the image of an overcomer. If I have a job in Corporate America and I came to you saying that I was a CEO or a CFO of a major corporation, and I came to you with my shoes run down and my hair looking messy and with wrinkled up clothes, you would be asking me questions. You'd be wondering where my iron and hairdresser were. Our problem is that some of us may look the part, but we don't have it on the inside. We have some ingredients missing. It's time for us to look the part and be the part. The way that God causes us to be the part is that He has to bust us down. He has to jack us on the left and jack us on the right. Why? Because there is an image that we are fighting against. We're fighting against the image of God. Romans 8:7 says, " Because the carnal mind is enmity against God: for it is not subject to the law of God, neither indeed can be." Carnality is synonymous with hostility. That means that when God says to go left, you tell God with an attitude that you are supposed to go right. How can you do this and say that you are saved and walking in His image? You are not. It's not until you can give up what you want for what He wants that you can say that you are truly walking in His image. Our problem is that we want what we want more than what He wants. We have to get to the place where we say for real for real what Jesus said in Luke 22:42: "Nevertheless not my will, but thine, be done." We love catch phrases. We love to sound deep, sanctified and religious. We quote things and tell lies. As soon as you get up you're gonna go where you want, you're gonna do what you want, you're gonna wear what you want, and you're gonna say what you want. We can't have the image of God and do what we want to do. We're supposed to be image bearers of the true and living God. I'm tired of this foolishness that we're calling the image of God. These nuts running around here calling themselves prophets, apostles and pastors that can't live holy. They are all attached and connected to foolishness because nobody showed them what the right image was. Just in case you didn't know, that is what God has been trying to do with us from day one. When Jesus gave His life, it was all about reconciling man back to God. With that reconciliation comes restoration of our right place, restoration of where we should be walking, restoration of the power of God, restoration of our authority, and restoration of our position. Position and authority go hand-in-hand. Let somebody come up and say they have authority but they have no position. We are going to look at them and ask, "Who are you?" You know who your supervisors are on your job. Let some nut come up talking about they are the boss for today. The only place they will be the boss is in their minds. Position and authority go hand-in-hand. We want authority, but we have to understand what our position in Christ is first. This is about us reflecting God. When He looks at us, He should be looking in a mirror. He should see Himself. This is the image of an overcomer.

The Lord said to me that the reason why some of us struggle with being overcomers is because we don't understand Revelation 12:11 which tells us that we will overcome by the blood of the Lamb and by the word of our testimony. We already know that we overcome by the blood. The blood is what gives us our position. But the word of our testimony is the word that comes out of our mouths, and the words that come out of our mouths are betraying us. We are saying one thing

131

and doing something else. What is your testimony? Your testimony is what you say out of your mouth. We already know that the blood has taken care of its part, but you have to get your confession right. James 2:12 says, "So speak ye, and so do". Stop speaking and not doing. Help us, Lord. We are going to go real quick to Romans 8:28, which states: "And we know that all things work together for good to them that love God, to them who are the called according to his purpose." It doesn't say that things work out according to our own purpose. It says that things work according to HIS purpose. How am I going to be an image bearer of God when I don't understand what my purpose is? If I pull the clock off the wall and try to use it for a plate, that's not what the clock was made for. There is a distinct purpose that we have been created for. If we do not roll in those roles and function in those functions, we are not fulfilling our purpose. You're here, but you're just taking up space. You're not fulfilling your purpose. If you don't know what your purpose is, you're just matter. You're inconsequential matter. Why? Because you're not making a difference in anybody's life. You don't even know why you're here. You can't just go to church talking about your mother made you come to church. You have to know your purpose. You've got to matter to somebody else. You have to know why you're here. Why are you here? Go back to Genesis and see why you're here. You can't say that all things work together for your good until you understand that you're called according to His purpose. You can't understand that until you know what His purpose is.

This word "purpose" is from the Greek word *prosthesis* which means "setting up". The things you're going through are going to work out for you because God is setting you up. It is going to work because He set you up. It was already out of your control. Your car breaking down was a setup, your bank account being overdrawn was a setup, hell breaking loose in your house was a setup - it was all a setup. You can rejoice and give God praise because you know it's not in your hands, it's in His hands.

I hear people say that they don't like blind dates. They don't like being set up by someone else because they don't know the person and they don't know what they will see when they get there. Some of us like to be in control. This is about God's divine design. His setup from the foundation of the world. Why am I here? Because I've been set up. This word involves purpose, resolve and design. God has resolved in Himself that this is what He wants you here for. He designs

133

you for His purpose and He wants you to fulfill His purpose. Because of that, when I have His mind, I resolve within myself that this is what God made me for, this is why I'm here, and this is what I'm going to do. I hope you are catching this. You have to know why you're here. This is the image of the overcomer.

We have to get our image right. We grow up in homes where mama slept with everybody. It was all about whatever the man's name was. And because of that, it messed up what we were supposed to do. When you look back in Genesis 5, something happened that when Adam gave birth to his son Seth, Seth bore his father's image. Seth was after the likeness of Adam. Remember that at this point, Adam had already fallen. Because he had fallen, what God is saying is that Seth grew up in a broke down and dysfunctional home. The likeness and the behavior that he saw was that of sin. He didn't model righteousness long enough that his children would be able to follow it when they were birthed out. When he had Seth, Seth bore the likeness of Adam and his sin nature. So we now have to fight against momma's devils, daddy's devils and great-grandma's devils. This is why you have to understand overcoming by the blood of the Lamb and by the word of your testimony.

My testimony and being able to overcome was rooted in understanding that every generational curse had to be destroyed. Had they not been destroyed, I would be dead today. How do I know? I can look back and the history will show me. I had to pray that the curses would be broken off my family. My grandmother had two kids: my mother and my uncle. Both of them are dead. My mother died at thirty-five. My uncle died in his early forties. One of my older sisters died at twenty-six. Everywhere I looked, it was death all around. I was like, "God, this cannot be my inheritance. This cannot be why you put me here. This cannot be what you have for me." I had to fight against the image and the likeness of what I was born into because I understood that the likeness that God had for me had nothing to do with whom I was born to. It had nothing to do with my mother and my father. One of my older sisters was murdered by her boyfriend. My father's baby sister was murdered by her ex-husband's ex-wife or something like that. These murders happened around twelve months apart. We had just finished one funeral for murder and went right back to another funeral for mother. I was watching these people die but I knew that wasn't for me. I didn't receive it and I didn't accept it. You have to understand that there's a fight for you to become the image of God. Life itself is

135

fighting against you becoming the image of God. Generational curses are fighting against you becoming the image of God. Society is fighting against you becoming the image of God. This world that we live in is all about conformity. The world wants you to look like the person that's sitting next to you and act like the person that's sitting next to you. The world expects you to have an attitude like the person sitting next to you. Loose here. I don't want any of that. We have to learn how to look into the perfect law of liberty and to become everything that God has created us to be. I'm sick and tired of not being able to see deliverance. The thing about it is that I know we see folks delivered, but to be able to see that, God is concerned about stuff that is not on the surface. It doesn't take a revelation to speak what is on the surface. You don't have to be a prophet to see what's on the surface. You don't have to prophesy to see what is obvious. But it's going to take revelation and having an ear to hear what the Spirit is saying to be able to understand that there is something on the surface, but there is something below the surface that caused what is on the surface. It's being able to see cause and effect. It's being able to speak deliverance to it. You have to get your ears tuned. Tune up. That is what you have to do to your car after you drive it for so long. Tune up!

We've got to bear the image of God. This is why we have such a hard time. The enemy is fighting against you becoming the image of God. He's fighting against you being able to understand that you are already an overcomer. He doesn't want your affection to line up with what God already said. You can't understand that all things are working together for your good because you don't understand your purpose. You don't understand the setup. Sometimes we look at the setup and we don't like it so we try to change it. No, just come on in and be a part of the setup. Some things we don't even have to put our hands in. Take your hands off. The Lord is saying that we have to overcome to the point that we understand purpose. Our purpose is to represent Christ in the earth. The reason why we sometimes overcome and then go back is because we don't understand our purpose. Sometimes God will deliver us from something and then a week later we're right back in it. Why? Because we didn't really get it. We didn't get it. This has got to go beyond a church service. It has to go beyond our gathering together. You have to have this thing in the Wal-Mart. You have to have this at the gas station when someone runs up to the back of your car and hits it. We had a thing happen while we were having a revival and one of the visitors made a mistake and hit the other visitor's car. The visitor whose car got hit was supposed to be an

137

apostle and he came in acting like was twelve. We need to grow up. Your image is locked in a Cadillac? What's wrong with you? That isn't the image. You look like it, but you ain't got it. You're missing something. Somebody didn't follow the recipe. There are some ingredients missing. I know we all have moments of weakness, but we need to cut this foolishness out. I don't want you being an apostle of a church if you can't be an apostle over your soul.

Image is everything. You can't force anybody to think anything but your nasty behavior will make them think something. This word "purpose" that is in Romans 8 also means "putting forth to be viewed on open display". God wants people to see you. You can't come out here representing Him if you don't have it together. Everybody wants to be out on open display, but they don't want to get their insides together. Until we get that right, God can't put us on display. You are making plans to do a takeover, but I'm going to need you to get right first. I'm going to need you ladies to not come to church PMSing. Men, you don't have ovaries, but some of you come in "PMSing" too. I need you to give your wife her ovaries back. This word also makes a reference to the showbread that was put before the Lord in the Scripture. What did they do with the showbread? They would put oil on it, and they would burn it. Sometimes people have to watch your house catch on fire. Do you know why? Because when you come through your recovery, and God is rebuilding your house and putting stuff back in place brick by brick, they will marvel at how He allowed you to recover. They will remember the bad state your house was in and they will see what God did for you.

We are overcomers, and we have to get our image right. Just like you wouldn't come out of the house half-dressed, you cannot come out half-dressed in the Spirit. It's important for us to have prayer lives, to read our bibles, and to spend time with God. This is why obedience is so important. When we are disobedient, we are not bearing the image of God. There is a song called, "You're on Display" that I just love. Guess what? We ARE on display. That's what the Scripture is saying. Jesus was on display but guess what? We represent Him here on the earth. We are ambassadors of Christ. We represent the Kingdom of God. Let me tell you something. The Kingdom of God is upside down when compared to this world. The world says that when all hell breaks loose, you have to sit down. Just because you suffer losses doesn't mean that God took His call back from you. Go back to the Scriptures. You've been set up. You didn't think He knew what was going to happen in life before you were even born? He knew from the foundation of the world where you would stump your toe and how many stitches you would need. You can't let a stumped toe keep you from doing what God told you to do. Rub your toe, get your stitches, walk away with a cane or limp, get yourself together and bear His image.

Romans 9:11 says, *"(For the children being not yet born, neither having done any good or evil, that the purpose of God according to election might stand, not of works, but of him that calleth;)"* God knew what was going to happen before it happened, and because of that, He still called you. He called you anyhow. He knew you would struggle with the image that He set before you but He still called you. He is not changing the image, but He's giving you time to get in it. He's giving you time to understand what your purpose is and what His will is for your life so that you can line up. God has a purpose. God has a resolve. God has a design. God has a will, and we must get our will in alignment with what He is saying. We are supposed to be bearing the image of God. We understand your gene pool. You may have facial expressions that look like your dad's or your grandmother's. But the real image is in the Spirit of God. The real likeness is in the Spirit of God. It is not a struggle to be who God created you to be because His seed is in you. His seed is in you. You can be who He says you can be. Life can come, situations can come, but we are still going to be who God says we can be. We've got to let this mind be in us. If I'm saying, "let", that means I'm not doing it. He's doing it. If I "let" you drive my car, I'm not driving it. You're driving it. You have to give up your mind and let His mind be in you.

Chapter Seven

Rahab: From a Ho to a Housewife

Joshua 2:1-21

"And Joshua the son of Nun sent out of Shittim two men to spy secretly, saying, Go view the land, even Jericho. And they went, and came into a harlot's house, named Rahab, and lodged there. And it was told the king of Jericho, saying, Behold, there came men in hither to night of the children of Israel to search out the country. And the king of Jericho sent unto Rahab, saying, Bring forth the men that are come to thee, which are entered into thine house: for they be come to search out all the country. And the woman took the two men, and hid them, and said thus, There came men unto me, but I wist not whence they were: And it came to pass about the time of shutting of the gate, when it was dark, that the men went out: whither the men went I wot not: pursue after them quickly; for ye shall overtake them. But she had brought them up to the roof of the house, and hid them with the stalks of flax, which she had laid in order upon the roof. And the men pursued after them the way to Jordan unto the fords: and as soon as they which pursued after them were gone out, they shut the gate. And before they were laid down, she came up unto them upon the roof; And she said unto the men, I know that the Lord hath given you the land, and that your terror is fallen upon us, and that all the inhabitants of the land faint because of you. For we have heard how the Lord dried up the water of the Red sea for you, when ye came out of Egypt; and what ye did unto the two kings of the Amorites, that were on the other side Jordan, Sihon and Og, whom ye utterly destroyed. And as soon as we had heard these things, our hearts did melt, neither did there remain any more courage in

142

any man, because of you: for the Lord your God, he is God in heaven above, and in earth beneath. Now therefore, I pray you, swear unto me by the Lord, since I have shewed you kindness, that ye will also shew kindness unto my father's house, and give me a true token: And that ye will save alive my father, and my mother, and my brethren, and my sisters, and all that they have, and deliver our lives from death. And the men answered her, Our life for yours, if ye utter not this our business. And it shall be, when the Lord hath given us the land, that we will deal kindly and truly with thee. Then she let them down by a cord through the window: for her house was upon the town wall, and she dwelt upon the wall. And she said unto them, Get you to the mountain, lest the pursuers meet you; and hide yourselves there three days, until the pursuers be returned: and afterward may ye go your way. And the men said unto her, We will be blameless of this thine oath which thou hast made us swear. Behold, when we come into the land, thou shalt bind this line of scarlet thread in the window which thou didst let us down by: and thou shalt bring thy father, and thy mother, and thy brethren, and all thy father's household, home unto thee. And it shall be, that whosoever shall go out of the doors of thy house into the street, his blood shall be upon his head, and we will be guiltless: and whosoever shall be with thee in the house, his blood shall be on our head, if any hand be upon him. And if thou utter this our business, then we will be quit of thine oath which thou hast made us to swear. And she said, According unto your words, so be it. And she sent them away, and they departed: and she bound the scarlet line in the window."

I have been reading this and God has been dealing with me about Rahab. He began to speak to my heart about us as women. One of the things that we have to realize is that there are things from my

143

past that will not leave us alone. There are things from my past that I thought I was over and finished with. I even thought that I was healed and delivered in my mind and my thought process. Yet, for some reason, those things just keep coming back. We may not want to admit it, but we are not as perfect as we look. In order for us to be faithful, available and teachable, we are going to have to deal with our issues. You are going to have to deal with all of that stuff that Jesus isn't in. You are going to have to deal with all the parts of you that have not yet been sanctified.

I began to look at Rahab and I did some study because I like to ready and study. One of the things that I noticed is that even the scholars have a problem with the promise that God has made to her. There is something about when a woman of God or a man of God understands who God is and goes to God and knows how to change God's mind. This is a serious thing. You have to understand that the story of Rahab does not stop here. We understand that as we keep reading, when you get to the sixth chapter you see that God had promised some things to her and as you continue to read in Matthew 1 and in Hebrews 13 you will see that she is recorded in the hall of faith. Even though she had a past, she did not allow her past to keep her from making a good choice to change her future. Sometimes we have mad bad choices over and over again and because of that, we seem to be stuck in a rut. Here she is, this woman who is a prostitute. We understand that she had her house up on the wall and this is where the spies went in. Joshua sent the spies into the city to go and see if they could take the city. As they entered the city, they went into the harlot's house. One of the things I love about this is that we always look at people that we know have had a past and we speak of what their past was. We itemize their shortcomings. These are things that seem to follow us and we don't know how to get rid of them. You're saved and you love Jesus, but you have stuff going on with you. This is what was going on with Rahab. What I discovered was that Rahab's boldness was not a coincidence. She was already searching for something and this is why the Lord allowed those men to come to her house. You have to understand that as you keep reading you will find that Rahab decided that she was going to leave her own people. She was a Canaanite. They were already given the word that they were supposed to kill everything in sight. They were not supposed to make a deal with her. She had sense enough to know that she was not going to let them get over on her. She was not going to help them out and then she end up dead along with her family. Rahab had heard about them before their arrival and she knew that it was time for her to get smart. Sometimes you have to sit down and think and make some decisions. One of the things I've found out about us women is that we know how to maneuver and get our families out of jams. Sometimes we get them out of things they never knew would have happened had it not been for us interceding and standing in the gap.

We find Rahab dealing with all of her issues. She's looking for happiness in all of these men. Rahab was a businesswoman. She wasn't just a prostitute; she was also an innkeeper. Her house was actually a hotel, so there were always people traipsing in and out of her house (not just men). She had a keen eye for real estate. She picked up the house and put it up on top of the wall. She had the rooms with a view. She knew that when people came to town, they would want to stay in her hotel. She was smart, but she was a prostitute. That was her negative. She didn't know how to do things in life without selling herself short. We have a bad habit of doing the same - settling for less than what God has ordained for us because we feel like we're not worthy of what God has for us. I've been reading a book called "Lean In" - it's not a Christian book. It's about the woman who is the CEO of Facebook. Some of the things this woman shares fits the mold for

146

some of us women, whether Christians or not. Our problem is that we have allowed everybody else to define who we are instead of looking into the Scripture and seeing who Jesus says we are. Just because Rahab was selling herself did not mean that it was all that she was. She had a desire for more, and some of us are the same way. We have a desire for more, but we don't know how to get it. We don't know how to get to that place where we can achieve more, do more, and be more. I'm sure that Rahab didn't have childhood dreams of selling her body when she grew up. I know that when we look at ourselves, we didn't say that we wanted to struggle or live on welfare when we grew up. However, there are times that decisions we make cause us to end up in situations we didn't realize we would end up in. Struggle will cause us to make bad choices. Struggle will make us think the wrong things about ourselves. Struggle will cause us to redefine what God says when He didn't really say what we said He said.

Rahab rightfully should have died. It was harvest season, so it was no big deal when the king's men came to her inn and saw all of the flax on the roof. They understood that the flax had to be dried out on top of the roof and it wasn't a big deal to them. She was able to hide the men under the flax. Rahab made the decision to help them and because she did this, her question was: "What are you going to do for me since I'm rescuing you?" Rahab understood that God was going to give them the city but she wanted to know what was in it for her. One of the things I like is that Rahab wasn't selfish. She needed the men to look out for her and for her entire house and everything connected to it. She wanted them to make sure that all of her family made it out alive with her. Because they made that promise, in the end, she became a part of the children of Israel. She was a "Ruth" before there was a Ruth. Their God became her God and their people became her people. The Lord set her up because she had better for her. When she married Salmon, he was one of the princes of the tribe of Judah. She didn't just marry a "nobody" - God gave her a good man who had some status. When they got married, they had a son and their son was Boaz. This is what you must understand: Rahab was supposed to be dead. Not only was she supposed to be dead, but they were already given the charge not to marry Canaanite women. God had already told the children of Israel, "When you get to this land, do not give your sons to the women there in Canaan. Do not let your people intermingle with them."

Let me give you a little history so that you can understand how powerful this is. This is a big deal. God gave the Law to Moses and there were people in the wilderness who died because of their disobedience to God's law. Here it was that because there was a woman who was bold enough to open her mouth and ask God for something that she knew she did not deserve, she found out that God had so much more than what she was asking for. What does that tell me? I can take you to the New Testament on that. The Bible says in Ephesians 3:20 that God "is able to do exceeding abundantly above all that we ask or think, according to the power that worketh in us." It's funny because we don't understand the power of intercession. We don't understand the power of us going to God and praying through. We don't' understand the power that God has put on the inside of us. How do I know? Because half of us don't pray like we should. If we understood, we would pray. Because we don't understand, we don't pray. We feel like it's too much.

When this woman has gone and lain with all these men, giving herself to them, you have to ask yourself where her mind was. What did she think about herself? There are some of us who may feel like we can't identify with her because she was a prostitute, but some of us grew up in homes where our mother said that we weren't going to be anything. Some of us grew up around brothers and sisters who said negative things to us that stuck in our heads and kept us from achieving what God said. Sometimes being in school and growing up being bullied by people caused us to grow up being timid and shy. Perhaps you had the reverse effect and now you are overly aggressive and ready to fight people as soon as they say something to you. Something had an effect on you somewhere. You have to understand what stigmas are. Have you ever had an experience in which God told you to minister to someone and you didn't want to do it for fear of what the person would say? Has God ever given you a word for your family and you did everything you could to convince yourself not to release it? You have to understand that there are too many things that are trying to tell you who you are. Because we don't get in the Word, we believe the lies of the enemy. We don't have to walk around half-dressed and shaking our behinds to get a man. God has more for us than that. As a result of us not understanding who we are, even saved people have stooped to the level of doing things they know they should not do. Why? Because they don't understand who they are.

I'm going to give you a little history real quick. Can I tell you my business? Well I will tell you a little bit. You might not be able to handle all of that. I wasn't a prostitute, but like Rahab, there were

150

things that were in me that made me make choices because I thought that was all I could do. I thought that certain things were all that I had. I worked what I had to work because I felt like it was all that I had to work. I knew I wasn't ugly so I felt like I could work it. When you get out in the business world and even in the church, there are so many stigmas and stereotypes. There are opinions about what we can and cannot do as women. There is so much stuff that the enemy has sent to try to keep us from being who we are. God knew what He was saying when He said that He would pour out His Spirit on all flesh and that sons and daughters would prophesy (Joel 2:28). He knew exactly what He was saying because He knew that somebody was going to be fool enough to believe Him. I have always had a big mouth. That's just who I am. You have to know your own truth and you have to own it. I was the kind of person that if I would lose fights in school, when I got home from school my sisters would kick my behind because I didn't' win or fight back. There was a time in my life in which I allowed people to bully me because I didn't know what I was fighting for. I had this one girl named Lisa and she used to bother me all the time. She would follow behind me and push me while I was walking home from school. She would curse me out and call me names. My friends would be trying to boost me up to fight but I wouldn't say anything. She was

151

at least six inches taller than me. I was not going to fight her because everything in me already told me that I was going to get my butt kicked. I need you to understand how we defeat ourselves before we even get off the starting line. All because I was thinking about what she looked like and I knew about her reputation, I was afraid of her. She knew I was afraid of her. I knew I was afraid of her. One day she came out again and she started bothering and teasing me. This time, something rose on me. I told her that I was tired of her messing with me and I told her that I was ready to fight. I was hollering and screaming. She was so scared that she just looked at me, turned around and walked away. She could not believe that I actually had the audacity to get the gumption to say that I was going to fight her.

There has to come a point in your life where you get sick and tired of being sick and tired of being sick and tired of being sick and tired! You have to get tired of taking the enemy's foolishness. You have to get tired of being labeled something that you're not. You will begin to stand up and be who God says you are. I'm in the place right now where I'm believing God for my entire family. Some people don't understand some things that are going on with our ministry but when I tell you that I have lost everything because I said I wanted to obey God,

I mean that I lost everything. This was a test for me that I had to actually ask the Lord if He was serious about. I am understanding, God will bring us to the place where the things we say out of our mouths will be tested. All of you wonderful saved people who say that you will go if you have to go by yourself, I want you to remember those words when you have to go by yourself. I had come to the place where the things that I was struggling with and losing made me question everything that God said. It made me begin to question everything that He said that I am and everything that I was supposed to do. You have to understand that there are many voices that will speak to you. Sometimes, it's not just the voice of other people. Sometimes it is the voice that is talking to you within that will talk you out of what God said. Why? Because your feelings are hurt. Because it cost you too much. Because it doesn't feel good at the moment. Because you look like a public spectacle in front of everybody else. You look like you don't know what you're doing. One thing I need to tell you is that as long as God is speaking to you, you had better obey what He's telling you to do.

What does that have to do with Rahab? I can identify with her. I can identify with the fact that it took boldness for a prostitute to take the men of God into her house. Those men of God took a chance because people were probably saying that Rahab had enticed them. If you read the Scripture, somebody knew that the men of God were in the city and they knew to go to the prostitute's house. I was looking at this and I kind of giggled to myself because the Young People Have a Saying, "You can't make a Ho into a Housewife." I beg to differ! Just ask Rahab! I have biblical proof that God can take a hoe and make her into a housewife. He can clean her up, sanctify her, give her a man of God and give her a godly lineage. God not only made her a housewife, He made her a Queen! This is proof that the mess you're in right now doesn't have to define you! What you see in your life right now, your limitations and your circumstances - are very temporary. You must refuse to allow your current environment to define you! I don't care if you're crying! You can't allow ANYTHING to prevent you from becoming all God says you are! You have to Believe God!! You don't have time to just be a "good girl". Good girls just make friends. You can't be trying to make friends right now! It's time to be fearless because it's time to make Spiritual History here! You must do what your mother couldn't do! You were born to do what your grandmother and your aunts, and other ancestors refused to do! Break the mold! Fulfill the will of God! Cancel the enemy's assignments against your bloodline! If you're not praying, start NOW! Walk away from the stigma and generational curses that have been thrown upon you, and like Rahab, enter into Covenant with God and save your whole family!"

What does this mean to you? This means that your time, your life, your circumstances and limitations are only temporary. You can't let any of your issues define you. You can't let that stuff tell you that you can't do what God said that you were going to be able to do. I don't' care if you're crying. I don't care who walks away from you. It doesn't even matter if you are blind, bedridden or bound to a wheelchair!! I will repeat this for you again. You have to believe God. I don't have time to just be a good girl! Good girls just make friends. Stop trying to make friends! Be fearless because YOU have to make spiritual history! You have to do everything that God has spoken for YOU to do. We ask God to let the fullness of His Spirit to come, but we don't want that. Those are just words unless you're willing to sell out and give up everything. Unless you're willing to look like a fool for the cause of Christ and for this gospel, you need to stop singing those songs because you're not singing from your heart. It's going to take a fearless woman to do what God is calling her to do. You are going to have to forget about your reputation. So what that everybody knows you have a big mouth? So what everybody knows you have a bad temper? So what that your family and friends talk bad about you. Maybe you don't have any friends. Who cares? The only thing that matters is God gave you a word. Nothing else matters.

There's a thing that they talk about concerning women in business. They say that women in business often feel like frauds. Fraud is willful deception for personal gain. The thing about it is that I could identify with that. I am telling you this because there are places where God will take you and things that God will do in your life that will cause you to sit down and question whether or not you have what it takes within you to do it. Why is it that if I go home and cook a good mean for my kids and they love it, we pat ourselves on our back and are excited, but if God uses us to bring deliverance to someone's life, we shy away from it as if we didn't' know we had what it took to get it done. There is something in us that makes us feel like we are fraudulent. There is something within that makes us feel like we're not worthy to carry our anointing. There is something within us that makes us think we can't do what God said for us to do. Why? Because we are like Rahab. We are living in our nice house on top of the wall but there is still stuff within us that causes us to go back and bring all these men to the house. You may not be bringing back natural men, but in the

Spirit you have opened yourself up to other lovers. Spiritually, you have opened yourself up to other thoughts and mindsets that don't come from God. You have allowed yourself to live in bondage and you told yourself that this was what God had for you. I was praying and I told God that my only desire for when this word came forth was that every mindset that is not like God would break off of you. I prayed that every reality that is not reality would break off of every one of our minds so that we could understand that we are everything God says we are.

Some things that we call humility are not humility at all. Some stuff, is just us beating ourselves up. I was in a service where someone sang a song, and when she was done, someone complimented on the awesome job she did on the song. She replied and said that it was God. The person said, "No, it wasn't God singing. It was you singing. YOU did a good job. God used you." We don't even know how to take a compliment. We throw ourselves under the bus. Now I'm not talking about walking in your flesh, but I'm telling you that if Jesus was not sure of who He was, when He got here, He would have never been able to stay up on that cross for you and me. You have to understand that. Your self-esteem and your identity are not rooted in this world. You have to tell yourself that you are not what the world says you are. You have to say that you are not going to let someone else tell you what you can and cannot do for God. If you see it in the Word, you can believe that you can do it. I'm crazy enough to believe that. It's time for you to break the mold. It's time for you to do what nobody else in your family has done. It's time for you to stop saying "God I'm coming" and go ahead and get there. It's time for you to stop making excuses for why you're not preaching when God told you to preach. You don't know what God has waiting for you.

I'm finding that some of us in the Body of Christ, as well as those who are without, are in need of serious and deep spiritual recovery. We have suffered losses and we have let those losses back us into a corner. Because we didn't look like other people or sound like other people, we thought that we were disqualified or illegitimate. You have to understand that God doesn't have any illegitimate children. I have a Daddy. I know where He is. I know how to get in touch with Him. He knows where I am. When are you going to decide that enough is enough? Some of you go home and you argue and bicker and fight with your family members and you just don't know when the end is coming. You come to church and nobody knows that you're going through some of the stuff you're going through. You've allowed all of the arguing and bickering and fighting to tear you up on the inside. You can't' even praise God like you want to. Some of you may go to church and cry and praise God and everyone will think that it's the power of God on you when in all actuality, it's the fact that you are broken inside. It's not the anointing. It's your brokenness. Your heart is grieved. Your heart is broken because your house seems like a bomb went off in it. One of the things I have come to realize is that the enemy has been going after all of our households and marriages in this season. I have been through to where my own children were not talking to me because I had to make a decision based on the Word and put my neck on the line. It cost me, but sometimes you have to do what you have to do. Following Christ is not about destroying family relationships, however, Jesus said that He came to bring a sword (Matthew 10:34). We don't believe the Word. We don't believe it.

It would be all right if it stopped there, but I have kids with big mouths like their mother. My business is all in Virginia, South Carolina, Florida, etc. Guess what? I don't care. If I had to do it all over again, I would do it all over again. Obeying God is worth every tear. You might not feel like you signed up for this but you did. When you gave your life to Christ, your life was no longer your own. You may have to walk by yourself and deal with being lonely. You will have to sit in crowds of people and feel like you're there by yourself. "She" hardly smiled, but honey "she" cried. I told the church that I was not crying at church. I may have cried before I got there, but when I got into the congregation of the mighty, I gave my God some praise. I've had to cry on my way to church and ask God to help me to get it together because I couldn't give the people my situation. I had to give them His Word. God is killing our flesh. He's stripping away everything that's not like Him so that nothing else is showing but Him. If you can't stand this stripping, you are not going to make it. This is serious. We all look good when we have our Spanx on, but baby when you take that bad boy off... Watch it wiggle... See it jiggle. We all have a little blubber that we're trying to hide. We put on our spiritual girdles when we come to church and we suck it up and we look cute. We look like we get it together. When we get home and let it all hang out, you're not looking at your husband saying, "God bless you"... You're looking at him saying, "Man if you don't shut up! I'm sick of you. You're getting on my nerves." Don't lie. I know you're not that sanctified. There have been some things that came up out of me during my testing season that I had to ask myself where they came from.

That's the honest truth. The Lord had to help me to see that it doesn't matter if you feel unqualified. It doesn't matter if you feel like you can't' do it. That's where God wants us to be. Paul said it really well when the Lord spoke to him and he was trying to get rid of his thorn. God said to him, "My strength is made perfect in weakness." (II Corinthians 12:9) It's not until we can't stand on our own that God steps in and stands up in us. Now I understand what David was saying when he asked God to make his feet like hinds feet (Psalm 18:33) because when I feel like I'm about to tip over, I can just lean back on the back of my feet. When I can't stand anymore, God gives me the grace to keep standing. I can redefine every boundary that has been set out there for me. I can do everything the enemy said I could never do. I can do everything that I told myself that I would never be able to do.

Let me tell you something. It is wonderful to have prophecies and promises from God. I have received many prophecies and God has spoken many things to me. But it's different when you begin to walk that thing out. That's when you are tested. As you begin to do what God is saying, something in you is saying, "Are you supposed to be doing this?" Everybody is telling you that you're doing a good job, but they have no idea what you're going through. That is the stuff I was talking about when I mentioned feeling like a fraud. I was reading some statistics about how men and women think differently. Some things are very spiritual, but there are some things that occur because of how we have been raised. Men are taught to be high achievers. Women are taught that their achievements should be in the realm of having children, being married, cooking and cleaning. Even in this day, this is still the mindset. One of my sons' think that is all his wife is supposed to do when he gets married. God bless... I hope you can find that. Now I'm not demeaning our roles. I'm saying to you that you can do that and more. I remember when the Lord began to speak to me about me preaching and traveling. I didn't know how it was possible because I had four children. As my children got older, I began to see the plan of God unfold. They are all grown now and doing their own thing. The plan of God is unfolding. You have to understand that you're not just alive for your children. I used to think that. We all grew up thinking that if we could just live to see our kids grow up and graduate from college and have a couple of grandkids, we would be fine. God has more for you than that. He has much more for you, but you have to hunger for more than where you are. If you're gonna be faithful, available and teachable, let's first talk about being available. Availability doesn't have office hours. God has more than office hours.

You are going to have to be available more than office hours if you are going to accomplish anything for God. You are going to have to be available twenty-four hours a day, seven days a week.

I want you to understand that you are not what everybody else says you are. You're not a fraud. You're not a poser or a faker or a wannabe. You are the daughter of the Most High God. I'm not trying to tell you to be proud of flesh and self. I'm telling you to tap into Jesus on the inside. There are great things that God has for you to do and He needs you to be able to realize that you can do them. If you are constantly saying that you don't' know how you're going to do it, you will never know how you're gonna do it. God sets things in motion. You have to deal with your thoughts. Proverbs 23:7 says that "as a man thinketh in his heart, so is he." You shoot yourself in the foot before you even get out there. You can't allow your struggles and family issues to keep you from doing what God said to do. The Bible says in Acts 14:22 "that we must through much tribulation enter into the kingdom of God." Much. Not a little bit. There may be things that happen to you that you may never dream would ever happen to you. You may experience pain like you have never experienced before. Don't give up on God. Don't tell yourself not to be available.

163

Recognize that God is teaching you how to trust Him. We can't blame others for where we are and where we're not. Some things are because of choices that we have made. Some things have been things that people have said and done to us, but we allowed those things to affect us in such a way that they crippled us. You have to be like Rahab was and be bold enough to ask for something that you're not entitled to. God will change a law for you. Yes, He will. God will change His law just for you if you believe Him for whatever it is that you need to believe Him for. It takes boldness. You will have to step out of whatever you think about yourself and what you think you can't do. You are gonna have to tell yourself that you can do all things through Christ that strengthens you (Philippians 4:13). It's not in your own strength anyhow. It doesn't matter how you look. It doesn't matter if you don't speak well. None of those things matter. The only thing that matters is that you believe God and that you do whatever it takes to stand on His Word and follow His instructions.

I want to share one last thing with you. I want you to think about this. The Bible tells us that it was harvest time when the spies went into the land. As I began to think about the fact that Rahab hid those spies under what was in her harvest, I realized that those men had come in and they were her deliverance. She didn't even know it until she asked. The Lord spoke to me and told me that for some of us, we don't even realize that our deliverance comes with our harvest. The thing that we have been believing God for and waiting for, the thing that God has promised us - there is deliverance coming with that thing. There is a new mindset coming with what He's promised. There's healing coming with what He's promised. You have to be willing to receive it. You have to understand that you are worthy of it because you are His daughter.

Chapter Eight

He Called Me Sarah

Genesis 18:1-15 (English Standard Version)

"And the Lord appeared to him by the oaks of Mamre, as he sat at the door of his tent in the heat of the day. He lifted up his eyes and looked, and behold, three men were standing in front of him. When he saw them, he ran from the tent door to meet them and bowed himself to the earth and said, "O Lord, if I have found favor in your sight, do not pass by your servant. Let a little water be brought, and wash your feet, and rest yourselves under the tree, while I bring a morsel of bread, that you may refresh yourselves, and after that you may pass on—since you have come to your servant." So they said, Do as you have said. And Abraham went quickly into the tent to Sarah and said, "Quick! Three seahs of fine flour! Knead it, and make cakes. And Abraham ran to the herd and took a calf, tender and good, and gave it to a young man, who prepared it quickly. Then he took curds and milk and the calf that he had prepared, and set it before them. And he stood by them under the tree while they ate. They said to him, "Where is Sarah your wife?" And he said, "She is in the tent. The Lord said, "I will surely return to you about this time next year, and Sarah your wife shall have a son." And Sarah was listening at the tent door behind him. Now Abraham and Sarah were old, advanced in years. The way of women had ceased to be with Sarah. So Sarah laughed to herself, saying, "After I am worn out, and my lord is old, shall I have pleasure? The Lord said to Abraham, "Why did Sarah laugh and say, 'Shall I indeed bear a child, now that I am old? Is anything too hard for the Lord? At the appointed time I will return to you, about this time next year, and Sarah shall have a son." But Sarah denied it, saying, "I did not laugh," for she was afraid. He said, "No, but you did laugh."

I want to begin by giving a commentary not about the first three verses. Sometimes, God comes to the place we live and we don't recognize that it's Him. As a result, we stay where we are instead of doing what he did which is to run out to meet Him. Abraham recognized that this was a visitation from the Lord. Sometimes we have to open our eyes and be able to discern when the Spirit of the Lord is moving in the midst of us and what it is that God is wanting to do in the midst of us. You don't realize that your answer has come to meet you but you didn't get up to greet it. You didn't recognize that it was your answer all along. You didn't recognize that the thing you have been praying for and asking God for had come to see you for a visitation. You are going to have to change your posture in this hour. If you are going to get what you want and need from God, you are going to have to learn how to get up from where you are. For some of us, we shy away because what we see don't look like God. We are so full of ourselves. We are so full of pride. God is coming to meet our needs and we are too lazy to get up. He lifted up his eyes and looked. He didn't walk, he ran out to meet them. That's saying something right

167

there. He got in a hurry about going to receive his visitation. You don't have time to be waiting on other people. You have to get up and run to the presence by yourself. This man had enough wisdom to know what to do. He wasn't thinking about where his wife was. Some of us can't function without our spouses. Some of us can't function unless we have a "boo" on our side. We have to be yoked up with someone and we need someone patting us on our backs. We need all of that superficial nonsense to feed our flesh. There is something about a man of God who loves the presence of God and knows how to recognize when God comes to his house. I'm tired of us women beating the brothers to church. When you say "shut-in", where are the brothers? Somewhere working on their cars? No, I need you to leave that car there and come and lie on your face in the presence of God because we need something from God for our house. I wish there was a man who would run to the presence of God. You are going to have to leave your macho and machismo to the side and come get in the presence of God. This man understood that there was something that he had been waiting for God to do. He knew that these men weren't just regular travelers. You know anointed men and women of God when they stand in your presence. It doesn't matter if we are all laughing it up or whatever, you know when someone is standing in front of you and they have been smeared in the anointing. You know when someone has been in the presence of God. They are not playing games, pulling punches or mincing words. They come about their business to handle God's business and then they're out. This is where we have to get back to because we have become too distracted with life. We have become so distracted with our jobs and our children and our spouses. Thank God for all those things, but you have to understand that God didn't put you here for all of that. That was extra. When you work on your job, you get paid to do your job. You don't get paid to use your benefit package. Your benefit package comes with the job. You can't take your focus off the job and start dancing about your package. That's what we are doing. Our blessings are a part of God's benefits package. We get all excited about our blessings and we forget about the Blessor. We forget about the God who saved us and who called us out of darkness and into light. We forget about the God who has changed our function from sinner to light bearer. We get sick and tired of being a light. That's why we have so many lukewarm Christians. That's why we have so many people who don't have a prayer life. That's why we have many people who don't want to come to church. They pick and choose when they come to church based on what they think is going on in the service. We need a corporate move of God. We need God to move on all of us at once.

So he went out, and not only did he go out to go meet him, but he bowed himself before them. That's a man of God. He said, "O Lord, if I have found favor in your sight, do not pass by your servant." This is the type of stuff I'm talking about. Even if you didn't come to church with the right spirit for whatever reason, you can still change your purpose in being there. He was not sure about whether or not he had favor yet, so he said "IF I have found favor in your sight, can I get you to linger here a little longer with me?" Can we just make God stop doing what He's doing so that He can come and hear what we have to say? The problem is that we're not hungry. Some of us don't really want anything. We're just here to be here.

He said, "If I've found favor, can you please just stay here? Can I show you some hospitality?" We don't even know how to treat the presence of God when it enters into a place. Some of us can't even lift our hands because we're laughing and talking, passing notes, sending text messages, and all of that kind of foolishness. You don't even realize that God is in the midst of you coming to bring your answer and you miss it. Have you ever missed a bus? God forbid that they're on a Sunday schedule and they only come once an hour and it's hot outside. Now you have to sit outside in the sweltering heat for another hour because you missed your ride. You missed the move of God so now you have to wait and see if God is going to trouble the water again.

Verse 4 says, "Let a little water be brought, and wash your feet, and rest yourselves under the tree." We should want God to come and rest with us. Jesus is still looking for a place to dwell. The Bible says in Matthew 8:20 that when Jesus walked the earth He said, "And Jesus saith unto him, The foxes have holes, and the birds of the air have nests; but the Son of man hath not where to lay his head." When Noah was in the ark, he had to let the raven out the first time and the raven didn't find any rest. The raven came back. When the ground really started drying up, he let the dove out and the dove found a place to rest so he did not come back. Do you get what I'm saying? God is still looking for a place to rest. You have to invite Him in. He's coming by, but you have to open the door. Some of us sit and look at the door trying to figure out who it is - it's your answer that you have been waiting for. Think about the promises that God has made to you that you are still waiting for. There is nothing like being in labor and not knowing how long you're going to be in labor. That's a bad feeling. God came with a timeframe to give you some relief and you missed your relief because you couldn't let Him in.

After we give God a place to rest and I receive of Him and I worship Him, then He can go and do what He's going to do - but I'm not letting God pass me by. I may not be the best singer but He likes to hear my voice, and as long as He likes to hear it I'm going to sing to Jesus. We have to learn that the anointing can fall through the cracks.

Verse 8 says that Abraham stood by the tree while they ate. He didn't eat. Imagine that you go and cook all of that food and then you don't sit down to eat. He stood to serve. We need to get a servant's heart again. We can't wait for someone to tell us to put our feet under the table. How about you serve? How about fixing someone else's plate for a change?

I want to turn your attention to verses 11-12:

'Now Abraham and Sarah were old, advanced in years. The way of women had ceased to be with Sarah. So Sarah laughed to herself, saying, "After I am worn out, and my lord is old, shall I have pleasure?"

I need you to say, "Lord, are you still going to do what You said You're going to do after I've been worn out?" I'm going to give you some history really quick. Sarah at this point has already gone through three transitions in her life. It would take history searching and background study to understand the transitions that she had gone through. At this point, God has already changed her name. When God changed her name it was not her first name change. Her first name change came as a youth. The historians say that Sarah was called "Yiscah" because on her they saw the presence and the anointing of God. She had a seer's anointing on her. Not only that, but it was also because she was beautiful to look at. That was her first name. As a teenager, she married Abraham. Before she got married, her name was changed from "Yiscah" to "Sarai" which means princess. However, "Sarai" means princess only in the terms that she would rule over her own house. Then she comes to the place here God changes Abram to Abraham and Sarai to Sarah. God says something to Abraham and to

173

Sarah, and He says the same thing twice. Even though Abram's name means "father of many", it only encompasses a few in number. Here it was that God changed his name to Abraham, which means "father of many nations". God called him something that he didn't even possess. You have to see this because there are times in which God is speaking something to us and we don't even have it. We don't even see it. When God changes Sarai to Sarah, her name means "princess par excellence". This is symbolic of the covenant that God made to her. God made a covenant with her stating that she was going to be an heir and that she would rein and have influence. It was not just going to be over her little tribe. God placed a global anointing on her that she didn't even know was there. The problem with this is that she was like some of us. She had too many issues. Although she had a husband who understood when he saw the presence of God approaching Him, there was a problem with his perception when it came to her anointing. That was her first issue. The other thing was that Abraham was a fearful man. Fear will make you do dumb things.

I'm going to give a little sidebar to the brothers. Brothers, those of you who are married need to know how to be secure in yourself. It is imperative that you understand that you have a kingdom assignment with your spouse. If you don't recognize that you have a kingdom assignment together, your insecurity will make her hide her identity. Can I prove it? The Bible says in Genesis 20 that as they traveled, Abraham came to a land and he told his wife to say that she was his sister. He needed her to hide because he didn't want everybody to know that she was his wife. He was afraid that the Egyptians would ravage her. We need to see some men of God who are not fearful. It takes boldness to stand and say what God said and do what God said. If the truth the sisters really want to follow. It is when the spirit of fear is seen that the women say that the men aren't going to do what needs to be done. I am not male bashing. The truth is the light. The reality is that because we won't tell ourselves the truth, the brothers aren't standing up and we need them to stand up. That is God's order for things. Because things are out of order, we can't see our children in position in the Kingdom the way they are supposed to be. I did say that Abraham loved the Lord and that he was discerning. The reality is that we need you to be a man outside of church. It's not too hard once you feel good in the Holy Ghost to get on the mic and say whatever, but even when you are at home, you have to set some things in order. I'm saying this because our families have suffered too long. God has spoken to us and we are in the position now where we have been worn out. However, God's promise still stands.

The truth of the matter is that life has worn us out and we won't tell ourselves the truth. We want someone to prophesy to us, but we want them to tell us what we want to hear. We don't want anybody to tell us that we are a hot, stinking, flaming mess. We don't want them to tell us that we talk too much and that we don't pray enough. We don't want them to tell us to exchange our gossip life for a prayer life. How is your unsaved husband going to come to God if you are not living a nickel's worth of dog's meat? You aren't praying when you are at home. We don't even see you crack your bible. We see you reading those nasty romance novels. I used to work at the library. I was a librarian, and I know that some of the saved folks would come in and get some of these nasty novels and take them home and read them. Then you wonder why when Jesus shows up you can't even address Him. Ladies, you have to get to the place that if you want someone to honor you for who you are in God, you need to learn how to walk there. Do it with humility. Take your fussing and pride and sit it down for a little while. Get some Holy Ghost. Learn how to talk to people. There are issues that we struggle with that we need to be honest about. I will give you an example from my life. We're riding in the car and I'm to the sisters about how I was studying temperament. I was studying my own temperament. We are so busy trying to get information on other people; we forget to study ourselves and our own issues. So I'm telling them about my study and how I know I have a strong personality. Sometimes I don't realize that I'm saying something when I'm not saying it. Has your husband ever told you that you have an attitude and then you reply back to him with an attitude telling him that you don't have an attitude? It's because we have been worn out. God's promise is still to you, but you have to deal with what has been worn out. Sometimes when we get worn out, we act ugly. I had to have an awareness about myself. I was reading a psychology book and I got convicted. I wasn't reading my bible. I was reading a psychology book. God can use whatever He wants to use when your heart is open. When you ask God to help you because you want to be what He wants you to be, He will use anything. There is stuff that happened in my life that wore me out and contributed to my temperament. So I give nasty looks sometimes and don't realize that I'm doing it. My neck (with my sanctified self) rolls sometimes. I have the tendency to look down at people over my glasses. We have to deal with our issues. I'm saying this to you because I want you to understand that God knows all about

177

our junk that we have in our trunk. It doesn't disqualify you, but He wants you to be honest about your junk in your trunk. He wants you to come clean about it. We have the tendency to be brutal. We can be honest without being brutal. You don't have to kill a person because you're being honest. Can we leave them with life in them when we're finished?

With some of the problems that we're experiencing, we think we're the victim when we're actually the perpetrator. Like Sarah, we're denying what we are really doing because we are deluded about ourselves. We lie and say that it's not us, when it is us. We know that we have this stuff. Three quarters of the arguments we have at home are because of looks we give and mannerisms that we have. Here's the thing: You are teaching when you're not talking. Look at your children. I have two that have attitudes that are out of this world. "Nasty" is putting it mildly. They are like this because they grew up with... me. Did I say that? Yes I did. I wasn't mean to them, but there were things that I was bruised about. There were things that I was worn out about. I love them. I prayed for them. I wanted them. But because I was wounded and because I was hurting, they have a persona. I'm telling you that God wants to do a healing in us. He wants to do a deliverance in us. I know what God wants to do for His people. There are things that we are worn out about that we don't even realize that we have been worn about. The answer has shown up to our house and all we think is, it isn't for us. When the Scripture says that Sarah laughed, it doesn't mean that Sarah thought what was being said was funny. She laughed because she mocked God in her heart. She couldn't even see herself as God saw her. He changed her name and she still could see who she was. God is telling you that He loves you. He's telling you that you will get everything He has for you, but you can't embrace it. You don't know how it's possible to have what God says you can have. You're worn out. You can't even think straight. Sarah couldn't process the fact that she was going to be a mother of nations because she couldn't have any babies. She was too old. She felt like she had missed her deadline. We feel the same way. "I missed my deadline. I waited so long. And now that I'm worn out, You show up?" EXACTLY. Now that I feel like I can't take it anymore, You show up.

Can I tell you something? What I'm finding out is that whenever we start really telling what God is delivering us from and people start getting free, the enemy gets mad. I went to a service and I had to preach and God moved for His glory. I was tired and my body was in pain. I had personal stuff that I was going through. I didn't say anything to anybody. I was sitting in my room with the door closed and I was just crying. I felt like it was too much. I looked at my pain meds. I had a fight in my mind about swallowing a bottle of pills. When we get to the point that we're worn out, the enemy makes us think it's over. God is saying that this is where He will show us His power. This is where He will show us His glory and that He is still God. He did it on purpose. You have to be like Abraham. You have to recognize your visitation. What if he would have missed it? What if the answer was coming to his tent and he didn't invite them to stay?

God is speaking to you today. Your answer is here. You don't have to be worn out. You don't have to kill yourself. I had to plead the blood of Jesus over my mind because I was worn out. If the enemy is doing that to me, I'm not in your house but I know you're going through. You have to understand that you are in the place where God wants to show you who He is. He wants to show you that He is still God and that He still sits on the throne. It's not too late. I don't care what everybody else said. I don't care how old you are. Sarah was eighty-five. If we look at the Scripture, we see that this is how God operates. He did the same thing with Lazarus - He waited for him to die. He's waiting for some stuff to die before He shows up because we don't really believe Him. We remind Him of what He said but then we don't believe that He's going to do what He said because we don't see how He'll be able to do it. Everything that He said you would have, you will have it.

I understand now what David meant in Psalm 27:13 when he said, "I would have fainted unless I had believed to see the goodness of the Lord in the land of the living." I would have taken those pills if I didn't get a hold of myself and let my faith come alive. If God said it, He has to do it. He has to. Sarah had a moment of insanity because she had waited so long. She lied because she couldn't deal with the fact that she really couldn't see herself as Sarah. Even though she had a prophecy hanging over her life from her childhood, she still couldn't see herself as God saw her. We see ourselves as no good and not good enough. Then when someone asks us how we're doing we say that we're good. Lying. Like Sarah, we are in denial about our issues. She answered when her husband called her Sarah, but she didn't believe that she was Sarah. There's a difference. You answer when someone calls you a man or woman of God, but you don't act like you believe it. You don't act like you have something in you that's worth looking up to because God is on the inside. We have been worn out. As children, we were worn up. We have grown up and now we are adults who are worn out.

Here we are with this promise, and God comes to visit us. What do you do? You're going to have to posture yourself to believe again. It's hard after you've been waiting so long. You know what God has said and you know what your purpose is. You know what He promised you, but you don't see anything. Everybody around you is in the same predicament. They don't see anything either. You're not the only one. It's not just that you can't believe for you - you can't believe because nobody else around you believes. You have to change your posture and you have to change your company. People who can't believe God with you need to step to the left. I'm coming to terms with me and I need you to come to terms with you. You have to believe that you are Sarah. You're answering to it - it's who you are. You're not just a princess anymore. It is princess par excellence. You are the model of everything God says "woman" is. That's what Sarah was. The Bible tells us in I Peter 3:6 that God will do for us what He did for Sarah if we are not afraid. I know how hard it is to believe God when you don't see anything. When you see absolutely nothing and all you have is what He said. I know what it's like when people say they believe God with you and they turn and run because God didn't move fast enough. They love us as long as we're blowing up, but if we look like we are deflating, they take off running. This is the same woman that out of desperation and lack of faith she gave her husband to a woman who turned on her (Genesis 16). God told Sarah that SHE was going to receive it. Isn't it something that when God promises us something, we try to push it off on somebody else? Have you ever tried to give someone else your responsibilities? He didn't tell them to do it. He said for you to do it. I'm guilty. I can't tell you what I didn't live. That's what I did. I pushed off my responsibilities. I heard Him call me Sarah but I didn't feel like Sarah. When I looked in the mirror I didn't see Sarah. I saw that I was worn out. I was past the time of waiting and I felt like I should have been further along. What does that mean exactly? I don't know but I felt like I should have been further along.

We have to start thinking and saying the right stuff. Proverbs 23:7 says "For as he thinketh in his heart, so is he." If God says your name is Sarah then you need to adjust your thoughts. A princess doesn't think like a pauper. You're not going to catch Donald Trump at some of these little huts where people cook. You won't catch him at a hole in the wall. Donald won't eat there. He eats at places where you have to wear a shirt and tie. If you are who God says you are, you have to begin to carry yourself a certain way. If you're not a "hoochie mama" then stop dressing like one. I understand that you might feel "hoochie" some days, but stay home. Don't take that outside. We can't wear everything. I know in your mind you're a size two, but honey, the mirror ain't lying. You aren't shopping in the petite section anymore. Don't be in denial. Can I tell you when I went on a diet? When I saw a picture of me. I said, "Who is that?" Then I said to the saints, "Why didn't y'all tell me I looked like that?" They were like, "Apostle, what was I supposed to say?" In my mind, I was a fourteen, but in the store I was buying twenty-fours. I had to come out of denial. Now I am a fourteen. Why? Because if you believe that you are something, start moving in that. You have to start moving in the direction of what you say you're going to be. If you're God's woman then go home and pray. Shut up, stop arguing with your husband and be ye quiet. My kids crack me up. When they get on each other's nerves, they say, "Do you want some shut up?" I know what that means. I don't want any. We have to deal with our impulsiveness. We make decisions without thinking and without praying because we're in desperation. When God

184

doesn't move when we think we should move, we go to our Plan B and C, D, E, F, G, all the way to Plan Z and when we're done it still doesn't look like what God said because He didn't say all of that. He didn't say that Hagar would be the mother of many nations. He said that Sarah would be.

I have to tell myself that I am Sarah. It doesn't matter whether or not I feel like I'm the princess par excellence. I'm going to present myself like I'm the princess par excellence whether I feel like it or not. You can't be a model until you start thinking like one. I'm not talking about a runway model; I'm talking about an example. You can't do that until you start thinking like one. We have to get delivered for these mindsets of being worn out. God has come to give you strength today. He has come to give you strength and to help you to get over you. We are our problem. Like Sarah, we have to overcome our shallow and carnal mindset. Some things we got through inheritance. Did you know that Sarah was Lot's sister? Lot was all caught up in what he could see. That's what got him in Sodom. Sarah was caught up in what she could see. When she looked in the mirror she didn't see Sarah either. She saw that she was eighty-five and dint' have a menstrual cycle anymore. We have to deal with our mindsets that talk us out of the promises of God before we receive them. How many times have you talked yourself out of what God said? We have to deal with this.

The other thing you have to understand is that after Sarah's death, Abraham took a seat. That told me that there was something that was in her that he realized that if she's not here, that's the end. Have we made ourselves indispensable? As a woman of God, who can say that their life is better off because you're there? Who can say that their life has been added to because you have positioned yourself to be who God says you are. After Sarah died, Abraham's ministry ended. He said, "That's it." He didn't want anybody else because she was the one. I'm not saying that you're about to die. What I'm saying is that you have to understand your value. You have to understand your worth. Proverbs 31:1 asks, "Who can find a virtuous woman? for her price is far above rubies." Honey, you are expensive. I want you to hear what I'm saying and don't get it twisted. A prostitute has the right mindset as it relates to people having to pay her to be with her in the sense that she understands that she's worth something. I'm not saying prostitution is right. I am saying that she understands that what she has is valuable and that if you want it, you have to pay for it. What I'm saying to you is that you have to understand that you have value and worth, and that you are too expensive to just give yourself away. You can't just hook up with people who don't have any type of education or goals. You can't hook up with men who want to sell drugs and hustle. You don't have time for that because you're going somewhere. God has a plan for you. If he isn't going anywhere, he is not a part of that plan. Ladies, don't settle. You're precious. It's more than just having a pair of legs in the bed. It's more than that. You need a man of God who goes after God.

Chapter Nine

Breaking Destructive Cycles

Let's begin by looking at Mark 9. Here you have Jesus and His disciples. Mark 9:14-29 (King James Version)

"And when he came to his disciples, he saw a great multitude about them, and the scribes questioning with them. And straightway all the people, when they beheld him, were greatly amazed, and running to him saluted him. And he asked the scribes, What question ye with them? And one of the multitude answered and said, Master, I have brought unto thee my son, which hath a dumb spirit; And wheresoever he taketh him, he teareth him: and he foameth, and gnasheth with his teeth, and pineth away: and I spake to thy disciples that they should cast him out; and they could not. He answereth him, and saith, O faithless generation, how long shall I be with you? how long shall I suffer you? bring him unto me. And they brought him unto him: and when he saw him, straightway the spirit tare him; and he fell on the ground, and wallowed foaming. And he asked his father, How long is it ago since this came unto him? And he said, Of a child. And ofttimes it hath cast him into the fire, and into the waters, to destroy him: but if thou canst do any thing, have compassion on us, and help us. Jesus said unto him, If thou canst believe, all things are possible to him that believeth. And straightway the father of the child cried out, and said with tears, Lord, I believe; help thou mine unbelief. When Jesus saw that the people came running together, he rebuked the foul spirit, saying unto him, Thou dumb and deaf spirit, I charge thee, come out of him, and enter no more into him. And the spirit cried, and rent him sore, and came out of him: and he was as one dead; insomuch that many said, He is dead. But Jesus took him by the hand, and lifted him up; and he arose. And when he was come into the house, his disciples asked him privately, Why could not we cast him out? And he said unto them, This kind can come forth by nothing, but by prayer and fasting."

Jesus had just come back from the Mount of Transfiguration, and He came down to meet the rest of the disciples. He had already sent them forth to go and cast out devils and heal the sick. The disciples then came upon someone with a devil they could not cast out. I think that every last one of us have come across a case that seemed to be very difficult. We have all come across hard situations that we have prayed about before but seemingly have not been able to get free from. When you get to the seventeenth verse, it talks about how the man has brought his son who had a dumb spirit. Now the King James Version cripples us because it does not give us the right transliteration. You really need to look at a Greek interlinear (word-for-word) mechanical translation to see what is really being said. Essentially, what the man is saying is that he was distraught because there were certain periods of time that would come and during those periods of time his son would start freaking out. It wasn't just that he was crazy all the time; it was that there were certain times in which the issue would flare up. These people were called lunatics because a lot of what they dealt with was in line with the phases of the moon. Whenever the moon would change, it seemed like the people would start going crazy. I still think that spirit runs through the land.

The man came to Jesus because he was distraught because he took his son to the disciples and they could not cast the spirit out. I'm not going to talk about casting devils out, but I really want us to focus on the fact that there are hard cases and hard situations that we deal with on a daily basis. It seems that we just can't break that bondage. You have prayed and asked God to help you and it seems like those things just won't leave you alone.

Number one, Jesus had to deal with their faith. Verse nineteen is interesting to me because we have a tendency to want to lean on all the strong people all of the time. Sometimes you have people who like to lean on the strong people. Here Jesus is saying, "I gave you all power and you still can't do this?" There comes a point in time where you yourself will have to get a devil up off of you yourself. You can't be sitting around waiting for pastor or prophet or anyone else. You need to be able to have a relationship with God yourself so that whatever it is you're going through, you can deliver yourself. I found out that we like coming to church and having hands laid on us. We like coming to church and having somebody prophesy to us. We like to come to church and have someone tell us what the Lord says. Wait a minute. When are you going to get by yourself and find out what the Lord said? Why do you always have to get secondhand information? I'm not fussing, but I am trying to tell you that we must deal with the fact that we are lazy in the Spirit. We like to lean on other people instead of getting our own relationship with God so that we can walk in liberty in Jesus' name.

I want to put a little commentary right here. This was the point in time in which this young man was about to get delivered. It seems like the closer you get to your deliverance, the worse your situation gets. It seems like the thing you're dealing with that you've been asking God to help you with seems to get worse the closer you get to it. Here this boy comes into the presence of Jesus and that spirit starts acting crazy. He is right at the point of his deliverance and then the devil starts trying to tear him. I found out that Satan just likes to get his last hoorah before he has to go! He has to act up one last time. He has to be crazy one last time. He has to try to get on your nerves by trying to make you cry one last time. He has to try to make you feel like God isn't going to move for you one last time. He does all of this forgetting that you are now standing in the presence of your deliverance. So tear me if you have to this one last time, but I'm getting ready to get free! It doesn't matter if it looks like everything is falling apart. It's just the enemy trying to have his one last hoorah.

The message that I want to talk to us about is about breaking destructive cycles. When you keep reading the text, it is just crazy because it's the same thing that happens to us all the time. The Scripture does not say anything about the spirit manifesting when the young man was in front of the disciples. The Bible says in the twentieth verse that when Jesus saw the boy and when the devil saw

Jesus, the spirit immediately began to manifest. I just want you to be encouraged because I don't care how bad it seems, how hard it is, or how much you have had to cry about it - you cannot forget that you are standing in the presence of God. You cannot forget that the One who is able to deliver you is standing in front of you and He is ready to deliver you.

For some of us, some of the things we have been dealing with are issues we have been dealing with since we were children. We're saved and we are delivered in some areas, but there are some things that have formed mindsets within us. There are some things that cause us to think a certain way and that if someone says the wrong thing to us it conjures up certain emotions because of what happened to us in our past. We start remembering all of what we have gone through and then we come to church and act like none of those things exist. We are full of ourselves and we need to stop it. I'm not saying we need to go to church and act like we need to lie on the psychologist's couch, but if you need the couch, take the couch. However, remember that we are in a deliverance moment and God is able to deliver us.

There are things that have been formed in us that because we are so accustomed to that just being our way, we don't know that these things are wrong. When I say "wrong" I don't mean that it's sin, I just mean that it's warped. We have a warped sense of thinking which creates a warped sense of behavior. Don't act like you don't know what I'm talking about.

One of the other translations says that from time to time the spirit would come upon the boy. I would call that an "anniversary spirit" - meaning that at a certain time of year, you always struggle with the same thing. Every single year in a certain month, here comes that same test. Happy Anniversary! We start dealing with stuff and we don't even realize our own patterns. Because we don't understand the seasons of testing and blessing, we find ourselves in these destructive cycles and we don't know how to get out.

So here is this boy, and his father realizes that this is a destructive cycle. There were different intervals of time that would pass and this demon would come and attack him. The father knew that he didn't have what it took to set him free so he had to find someone that could do it. Now I'm not against getting help, but I'm going to need for you to try to do the work first. When you find that you can't do it yourself, then you need to seek some help. This is what this man did. Jesus understood that this was a generational bondage. This was a bondage that had locked a hold of him since he was a child. If it came on him as a child that means it came from somebody. A lot of stuff that we're dealing with came from somebody. I know that you love you, but I am saying that you need to look at you. I had a conversation with my husband and I was telling him that for the previous couple of months I'd had a chance to sit down and look at and pray about some things. God had begun to allow me to see some things, and I found out there were some things I had lost myself in and didn't realize that I was lost. It's a bad thing to be someplace and not know you're there because mindsets set up in you. Things happen to you and you decide that you are going to protect yourself because you don't want to be bothered. We set ourselves in destructive cycles. So today I will be your friend but tomorrow, if the moon changes, we might not be friends. We have to deal with where we are. Everybody has some junk. I don't care how saved you are, you have junk. You can put all the perfume on that you want, but your boo-boo still stinks! Our problem is that we have come to church and we have felt good, but we didn't get anything. We even got a word, but we didn't get anything. You have to let that word get down in your spirit. You have to let that word begin to destroy the works of the enemy. You have to let it destroy things you got from grandma and momma and daddy. I have

195

my daddy's temperament and I am praying for my deliverance. My father is the type of person that would just want to blow everybody's brains out. He rides with his guns in his car. He is a straight up New Yorker and he doesn't care. He will kill you if he has to. That was my mentality. Even with the conversation I was having with my husband, there are things that cause us to get in survival mode. We often don't even realize that we are in survival mode. It's not that we're not trying to be bothered with anyone else; it's just that you are in survival mode. Because you're in survival mode, you're not letting anybody else really get near you. How many people have we pushed away because we were in survival mode? They were really good for us, but we didn't want them. How many friendships have you lost because you were in survival mode? You have to learn where some of this stuff is coming from. Some of this stuff comes from when you were a child, and you have to ask God to deliver you and set you free.

I'm not trying to talk anything crazy, but this is our reality. Because we come to church and we don't get delivered, we don't reach out enough for a tangible presence of God. We settle. We come to church and say that everything was nice, but we leave with nothing. No transformation. No change. Nothing challenged you and made you want to dig deeper and find out what God wants from you. I have been spending a lot of time with the Lord, and I've been asking God to show me what I need to do. We pray for everybody else but we don't pray for ourselves. We pray for God to save all of our unsaved loved ones, but we don't pray about ourselves. What about you? Are you praying and asking God about whatever is going on with you? Our reality is that sometimes we are too strong. Yes, you are strong, but there is nothing wrong with having a vulnerable place. Everybody needs to have someone that they feel safe with. Sometimes, you not feeling safe, is just you not feeling safe. It's not always that nobody is there for you. Sometimes it's that you won't let anyone in because you are strong. We watched mama struggle. We watched grandma struggle. We look at the news and see sisters struggle and we make up in our minds that we are not going to struggle like that. We don't feel safe with anybody. These are destructive cycles.

We have to be able to deal with where we are and what's going on with us. We have to deal with how we really feel. We always talk about keeping it real, but why don't we do that when we talk about what we're really dealing with? Now we say we're gonna keep it real when we're telling someone off, but when you are supposed to be talking about what's really eating at you, can you keep it real then? Truth be told, we are like this boy in the fact that every once in a while that cycle comes around. Whatever it is that comes to torment us shows up and says "Happy Anniversary... I'm coming to visit you again. What are you doing? What have you done since the last time I was here?" Because we have gotten so accustomed to the cycle, we don't cast the devil out. We sit down and have dinner with him.

Sometimes we just have to make sure we are okay. We are everybody else's caregiver. We take care of the kids. We take care of the husband. We take care of other people's kids. We're superwoman. We bring home the bacon and fry it up in a pan. But meanwhile, we're dying inside. Meanwhile, the moon has changed, and you have fallen down in front of Jesus while this spirit begins to tear you. Meanwhile, you're still struggling with whatever it was that made you feel like you were worthless. You're struggling with whatever it was that made you feel like nobody wanted to be bothered with you. We don't say stuff like that out loud because we're strong black women. Now I'm not coming against that; I'm just saying that when we do that, we think it's not okay to cry or show any weakness. That's not strength. Strength is to be able to experience all of that and still keep going. I remember one time praying and I was getting to the point that when I would ask God to deliver me from my weaknesses, I couldn't even get the word out. I didn't even want to say that I had weaknesses. There are things that you just can't do on your own. You need somebody else. If you didn't need anybody else, you'd be on a planet by yourself.

It's going to take faith to get out of these cycles. Keep in mind that you're not the only person who has gone through things like this. You're not the only one who feels hurt and doesn't always want to be bothered. You're not the only one who feels like they can be in a room full of people and still be lonely and alone. You're not the only person who has inner struggles. Even for some of us who are married, our cycles have hindered our marital relationships. We are so strong that we don't allow our husbands to know that we need them. I used to have it so bad. When my husband and I first got married, he was stationed over in Germany. The person who was supposed to be taking me to the airport didn't show up like they were supposed to. I ended up having to get on the plane without my bags because my bags were at this person's house. That meant I meant overseas with no clothes except for what I had on. He's my husband. He wanted to buy clothes for me. I didn't want him to buy anything for me, not even underwear. We got into an argument about him buying panties. He said to me, "Excuse me, I'm your husband. I've done seen your underwear. Let me buy some." There is something in me that didn't want him to spend his money to buy my clothes. I felt more comfortable taking money from the sisters in the church than to have him buy me some underwear. I was just willing to wash out the clothes I had on. That's how bad it was. There are things that are engrained in us from childhood.

I don't know what your story is, but my story is that when I was thirteen my mother died. From that point, I was on my own. I had to fend for myself. I learned the reality of how people can be when you have nowhere to go. I learned how to stretch a dollar. I learned how to shop. It wasn't that I wanted too - I had no choice. When you are in survival mode, you grow up in survival mode and then you live in survival mode every single day. It's not like a switch you can turn off and on - it's where you live. Some of us are the same way. Things have happened that have made us into who we are. Therefore, where we really are strong has caused difficulty in our relationships. We don't really who we are. I preached a message about how God had changed Sarah's name from Sarai to Sarah. Even though she answered to the name Sarah, in her heart she didn't feel like Sarah. She was waiting on promises from God to come to pass and she felt like it was taking too long. She was tired and worn out. Our lives have become that way. This is why Jesus asked His disciples where their faith had gone. I don't care who molested you. I don't care who beat you up when you were little. I don't care who mistreated you and made you feel like you were less than. Guess what? That is not the legacy that God wants you to leave in the earth. That's not who you are. Those are realities that have to break off of you. If you're ever going to be all that God says you are, you are going to have to look at those things and figure out how to get rid of them. I can tell you how: get to the feet of Jesus.

I began to look at the Scriptures to find some women who were stuck in cycles and unable to get out. Let's look at Genesis 27:1-7 (ESV): "When Isaac was old and his eyes were dim so that he could not see, he called Esau his older son and said to him, "My son"; and he answered, "Here I am." He said, "Behold, I am old; I do not know the day of my death. Now then, take your weapons, your quiver and your bow, and go out to the field and hunt game for me, and prepare for me delicious food, such as I love, and bring it to me so that I may eat, that my soul may bless you before I die. Now Rebekah was listening when Isaac spoke to his son Esau. So when Esau went to the field to hunt for game and bring it, Rebekah said to her son Jacob, "I heard your father speak to your brother Esau, Bring me game and prepare for me delicious food, that I may eat it and bless you before the Lord before I die."

We see here that Rebekah was the one who heard. Rebekah was Isaac's wife. Isaac was getting ready to bless his son and Rebekah heard what her husband said. She knew about the generational blessing. She felt like she knew who really deserved the blessing so she decided to get in it. How many times have we intervened and gotten into stuff that we should not have? Mommy, how many times have you gotten involved in your kids' business when you should not have? Rebekah became the manipulator because she just couldn't leave it alone. It wasn't that she wanted to be a manipulator; she couldn't help but meddle. There have been things that have happened and my husband would say to me, "Well why couldn't you just let it play out?" I felt like I had to handle things because I felt like he didn't know what he was doing. That's what we think, just like Rebekah. There are some things you don't even have to mess with. There are some things we just need to back up, leave alone, and let God handle. That's one of those things that have to break off of us. A lot of that comes from how we grew up. Our mothers meddled in everything and dared anybody to say anything about it. So when we grew up, we did the same thing. Even though my mother died when I was thirteen, my grandmother was still alive and I learned some of her ways. Help me Jesus. Even down to how I keep a house, my grandmother's ways influenced me. Sometimes I have to fight that. I can't stand for dishes to be in the sink. When I'm sitting down eating, I'm thinking about dishes. I can't even relax sometimes. Everybody else is sitting down and having a good time, and I'm thinking about cleaning the kitchen. We have to learn how to let stuff go. Who's going to die and go to hell because there's a dish in the sink?

Let's go to Genesis 31:19 (ESV): "Laban had gone to shear his sheep, and Rachel stole her father's household gods." So we have Rebekah the manipulator and Rachel the kleptomaniac. She couldn't keep her hands off other people's stuff. Saved, sanctified, filled with the Holy Ghost, and stealing. Always messing with people's stuff. Why did she feel like she had to take those gods from her father? Maybe you didn't steal, but the there are things in us that should cause us to want to ask God to let us see ourselves in the mirror. One of the things I always say is that the mirror doesn't lie. You might not see that you left a piece of meat in your teeth, but if you go to the mirror, the mirror will show it to you. You may not be able to see that you have a piece of hair out of place, but if you stand in the mirror, the mirror will show it to you.

Numbers 12 tells us about Miriam, the jealous psalmist who was greedy for power. She wasn't satisfied with the position that she had and she wanted to do something else. She decided that she was going to fight Moses. Everybody knows about Jezebel, the wife of Ahab found in 1 Kings 16-18. Calling someone Jezebel is like cursing in the church. She was the wicked queen of Israel and the enemy of God's prophets. She was a manipulator, a murderer, and a supporter of pagan worship. In other words, she just walked in her flesh. There are days in which we just walk in our flesh and do what we want to do. You may not have a gun or a knife, but you kill people with your tongue. We have the tendency to be abrasive. It makes you stronger to be able to hold your peace opposed to giving somebody a piece of your mind. Keeping your piece of your mind to yourself is what makes you strong. That's what the Holy Ghost is for. I'm not saying that we are terrible and horrible women. What I am saying is that when we are in certain situations, these things get magnified and it causes us to miss our blessing. It causes us to miss that blessed place that God has for us. Yes, we are virtuous women. We are everything that God says that we are. But one of the things I found is that the closer you get to God, the more the demonic stuff you have will start showing up. Do you want to be like Jesus? When you keep getting close, He will start showing you stuff. Can you handle what He's going to show you? Can you handle that sometimes we just talk too much and to the wrong people?

Ahab and Jezebel had a daughter named Athaliah (2 Kings 8-11) who was worse than her mother. This stuff went from generation to generation. Not only was she a murderer like her mother, but she killed her own family because she wanted to be the queen. She killed them all except for Joash. Thank God that somebody hid him. We have to be able to come against and destroy these generational curses of mental and physical illness. We have to come against these constant financial difficulties. Why don't we ever have any money? Because we gave it to McDonald's, Burger King, and Hibachi Grill. We sow more to our gut than we do to anything else. Help us Jesus. We have anger issues. We are ready to pop off in a heartbeat. We go straight ghetto in 2.3 seconds and it's not hard for us to do so. Let someone cut you off while you're driving. You'll say everything but a cuss word.

You might as well say it because you thought it. We have anger issues and irrational fears. We fear things that aren't even going to happen and don't even make sense. We just can't handle stuff. We get scared that people are not going to endure with us. We can't have good friends because we're scared and we scare them away. We feel like we have to bust them up before they bust us up. Self-sabotaging behavior. Ladies, we have to get delivered because these things are hindering our relationships. God is still going to use us, but there are things we have to come to terms with. All these years dealing with these bondage, and you're still not free? It's only because you didn't acknowledge it. You got used to the cycle. You're grown to already know what to expect when the moon changes. You have to get in your heart that you want to be free. You have to purpose that you're not going to let anyone or anything keep you from what God has for you - not even you.

We have to get free because we are passing our bondage off to our children. What we see them doing drives us crazy because we are looking at ourselves. Ouch! I have four children so I know what I'm talking about. I can see some of the things I did and some of the mindsets I've had in them. This is not just about you getting free; it's about your family being able to get free. It's about who is watching you so that they will be able to get free. From this day forward, I don't care who was locked up in a mental institution - it won't be you!. God has given you a sound mind. It doesn't meant that you won't have days where the enemy will try to remind you about your past behaviors. You have to learn how to get with somebody and tell them the truth. If we work on this, we will have better relationships with our families. We will have better relationsh8ips with our husbands. We will have better relationship with our friends. I'm not saying that relationship issues are all your fault, but I am encouraging you to take responsibility for your contributions to them. You take responsibility for whatever mindsets or bondages that you are dealing with. Be honest with God. I have had to say some things to my husband that I never felt comfortable saying. In my mind, he just should have known it. He's not a mind reader. We have these expectations and when these expectations are not met, we are disappointed and we catch an attitude. We cut people off. We have to deal with that. Why are we trying to make everybody read our minds? I had to tell him that I had a hard time talking about how I really feel deep down inside. I think it's unfair for us to be in relationships and expect people to read our minds. That is too much work. They are not going to get it right. They are not going to be able to catch everything. You are going to have to be able to feel free enough to say whatever is in your heart.

We have to understand that the power of God is in His Word. It's not in the shake and the noise. His Word is so powerful that it doesn't have to be screamed across the room. We can whisper His Word and chains have to fall off. We can just declare His Word and freedom has to show up. His Word is powerful. He wants us to get to the place where we rely on His Word more than anything else. Don't rely on your shout. Don't rely on the preacher tuning up. That's not what will free you. What's going to free you is what's coming out of this Word. This Word is spirit and life (John 6:63). If there is something in you that is dying on the inside, speak life to it.

Let's look at Isaiah 61:1-7 (King James Version):
"The Spirit of the Lord God is upon me; because the Lord hath anointed me to preach good tidings unto the meek; he hath sent me to bind up the brokenhearted, to proclaim liberty to the captives, and the opening of the prison to them that are bound; To proclaim the acceptable year of the Lord, and the day of vengeance of our God; to comfort all that mourn; To appoint unto them that mourn in Zion, to give unto them beauty for

ashes, the oil of joy for mourning, the garment of praise for the spirit of heaviness; that they might be called trees of righteousness, the planting of the Lord, that he might be glorified."

"And they shall build the old wastes, they shall raise up the former desolations, and they shall repair the waste cities, the desolations of many generations. And strangers shall stand and feed your flocks, and the sons of the alien shall be your plowmen and your vinedressers. But ye shall be named the Priests of the Lord: men shall call you the Ministers of our God: ye shall eat the riches of the Gentiles, and in their glory shall ye boast yourselves. For your shame ye shall have double; and for confusion they shall rejoice in their portion: therefore in their land they shall possess the double: everlasting joy shall be unto them."

There is a liberty that belongs to us. Because of where we grew up, whom we grew up with, and all of the stuff we have had to face, we have not been able to embrace that liberty. We walk around wounded and hurt and never really telling people who we really feel. It usually comes out some kind of way, usually the wrong way. God wants us to be able to understand that today is about Him binding up our broken hearts. There are things that have happened to us that we have not gotten over. There are some things that have wounded us that we should have been over, but just the thought of it brings us to tears. There are things that are broken that we have not allowed God to heal. What I found out is that there is a security in bondage. I can count on it. There's security in bondage. My bondage wakes up with me. My bondage goes with me to Wal-Mart. When I lay down at night, bondage is there. Bondage will never leave me nor forsake me. There is a security that we have grown to trust in that bondage. We lean on those emotions that have us wrecked in our minds and in our spirits. God is saying that He wants us to let that stuff go. It's hard to let it go because it's our night-light. It's our teddy bear and our thing that comforts us - but it's really not comfort. We have tricked ourselves and said that we're okay, and we're not okay. Who's going to take care of the caregiver if the caregiver is injured? Who is going to heal your broken heart? How are you going to heal someone else's broken heart if you're broken? How are you going to help someone else if you're in need of help right now? How am I going to pray you through whatever you're going through if I can't even get a prayer out myself? How can I dry your crying eyes when I can't stop crying myself? We have to go to God and say, "Lord, I need you do to this in me. You said that you anointed me to bind up the brokenhearted. My heart has been bleeding.

I need you to bind this up because I can't live if my heart keeps bleeding." There are things that people have said and done to us, and while we go on acting like it's okay, it is not okay. We are broken over it and we haven't been able to get over what happened. You say you're over it, but every time someone says that person's name it's like someone takes a knife and twists it inside of you. It hurts you all over again. It's not until you don't feel that anymore that you know that you've really been healed.

There is nothing like being free after you've been bound. There is nothing like being bound in one place and then being able to get up and walk around. That's what God wants to do for us. We have a great responsibility. We are birthers and nurturers. It behooves us to get healed and to let God deliver us because we are the ones everyone is counting on to birth them and to nurture them. We can't do it if we're still bleeding. We can't help anybody if we don't help ourselves first. Have you ever been on an airplane before? The flight attendant goes through the safety presentation and tells you that in the event of an emergency you need to put your mask on first before you help anyone else. What good is it for me to give you oxygen if I'm dying and unable to catch my breath? Put your mask on. Catch your breath.

Then come help me. Then come help your sister. Then go be a better wife and a better mother. Be a better grandmother and a better sister. You have to put your oxygen mask on first. Liberty is what God has ordained for us. On one hand God is coming to proclaim that this is the acceptable time. Why not today? Let today be the last time that you carry that brokenness and wounded heart. Today is the acceptable day. On the other hand, this is the time of vengeance. God is going to take care of whatever brought you to that position. You don't even have to worry about it. He will fight your battles and defend you. He will work out your circumstances and situations. It's time for us to really be real. Be serious about being real. Quit coming to church and playing games - acting like we have it all together but knowing that we are broken and beat up inside. Today is the last day. It is the will of God that you have a loving relationship with your spouse. You should feel safe with him. He is not everything you want him to be, and neither will anybody else, but we as strong women have to learn how to open the door and let our husbands in. They like to feel needed and respected. If they say that they don't feel needed and respected, recognize that it is their perspective. It is what he says about what he feels. If your kids say they need space, give them space. That is their perspective. Listen. That was hard for me. It is hard for you to not feel like you're being attacked. We feel like we are doing what we need to do and making sure that everybody is taken care of, and we get offended when things like that are said to us. Back up and give space. Just because you know how things should go doesn't mean that you have to do everything. Today is the acceptable day of salvation and deliverance for us if we want it. You don't have to have music playing. All you need is a heart that is ready to receive what God has said. It is as simple as that.

.

Chapter Ten

Get Your Head in the Game

Before we get into the meat of this chapter, you know we have to first get our minds wrapped around what God's Word has to say. IF we are going to get our minds right, it's only going to happen as we allow our thoughts and minds to be transformed by taking on the mind of Christ through the studying the Scripture and meditating on it. With that in mind, let's go to the Word.

Matthew 6:24-34

"No one can serve two masters, for either he will hate the one and love the other, or he will be devoted to the one and despise the other. You cannot serve God and money.Therefore I tell you, do not be anxious about your life, what you will eat or what you will drink, nor about your body, what you will put on. Is not life more than food, and the body more than clothing? Look at the birds of the air: they neither sow nor reap nor gather into barns, and yet your heavenly Father feeds them. Are you not of more value than they? And which of you by being anxious can add a single hour to his span of life? And why are you anxious about clothing? Consider the lilies of the field, how they grow: they neither toil nor spin, yet I tell you, even Solomon in all his glory was not arrayed like one of these. But if God so clothes the grass of the field, which today is alive and tomorrow is thrown into the oven, will he not much more clothe you, O you of little faith? Therefore do not be anxious, saying, 'What shall we eat?' or 'What shall we drink?' or 'What shall we wear?' For the Gentiles seek after all these things, and your heavenly Father knows that you need them all. But seek first the kingdom of God and his righteousness, and all these things will be added to you. Therefore do not be anxious about tomorrow, for tomorrow will be anxious for itself. Sufficient for the day is its own trouble."

I'm here to challenge your theology. One of the things we have to bear in mind is that we have a way of thinking that we have adapted from this world. We think that it is God's mindset but it is not God's mindset. We are going to go over a couple of things tonight and pay attention to what Jesus is speaking to His disciples. Basically what Jesus is saying is that we are looking at all of the things the Father created in nature. We see how God provides for them, makes ways for them and looks out for them - so why are we tripping? So what your bill is late? Why are you tripping? You have to know in whom you have believed (2 Timothy 1:12).

We are going to talk about going after the Kingdom of God. We're not talking about the kingdom of this world; we are talking about the Kingdom of God. I'm not talking about church membership. Thank God for church membership, but we are talking about the

Kingdom of God. If your eyes and your heart aren't fixated on the Kingdom, your church membership is useless. You are not going to do anything but get on your pastor's nerves anyhow because you don't have your mind on the Kingdom.

I want to dwell on verse 33: "But seek first the kingdom of God and his righteousness, and all these things will be added to you." This verse implies that God has a way that is not like our way. This verse implies that everything you think you know just could be wrong. I'm going to give you a couple of definitions because I am a teacher by nature.

When we talk about the word "seek" it implies that you are actively searching for something. Each of us has something that we are seeking after. That's what brought you to Jesus. You were looking for something. You had emptiness and a longing in you. There was something that was in your life that let you know that there had to be something else out there. You began to seek for something else.

Jesus is dealing with the appetites, desires, and drives of the people who are walking with Him. He knew that they were seeking after something, but He wanted them to begin to seek after the right something. He wanted them to start seeking after the Kingdom of God.

The only way that He could get them to start focusing on the Kingdom was to first deal with the fact that they were seeking after things. You have to remember that Jesus had people following Him that at one point had jobs. He didn't give them an explanation. He just said, "Follow me." If Jesus came to you today and said, "Follow me" wouldn't you be thinking about how you are going to pay your bills? We cannot see past today. We have our focus on the wrong thing. Jesus had to challenge them. Something that intrigued me is that in Chapter 5, we see that when Jesus saw the multitude, He went up to the mountain. When I began to look at that, the Lord began to tell me that He had to take them from low ground to higher ground to give them a similitude of what He was getting ready to give them. He needed to take them physically from a low place to a high place so that He could talk to them about high things. You know how we do. Things make better sense to us when we have natural correlations. Jesus was dealing with the fact that 'the seek' they had needed a focus. It's all right for you to be passionate and zealous. It's okay for you to be a go-getter - but what are you going to get? What are you passionate about? What are you zealous about? Are you using that same zeal for the Kingdom of God? Mind you, we have already established that we are not talking about church membership. In reality, some people feel like the Lord is talking to them and they don't have to do what their pastor says. The devil is a liar. You have to be able to be subject to the man or woman of God, and as the word of God comes to them they will share with you what the Lord says. That doesn't mean that you don't have the Holy Ghost, but you have to understand that there is one leader in the house.

God wants to deal with your seek because it needs a focus. We are led or driven by that which we seek after. Jesus has come to encounter us and He wants us to encounter Him. He wants us to change our focus and begin to seek after Him. I want to go back and look at some of these verses. I know that they say that we are in a recession, and I am not in denial of the fact that the economy is difficult. I'm not in denial of the fact that people are having a hard time finding and maintaining jobs. But what I am saying is that when you have a kingdom focus, you're not so much worried about what's going on in this world. This world is not your home. The problem is that we are setting up shop like we're gonna be here forever. We forget that Jesus is coming soon. We forget that the Bible says in 1 Peter 2:11 that we are pilgrims. This means you are a sojourner. You don't live here. You're a visitor. I live in North Carolina. Picture me acting like I live in New York. Reality waits for me in North Carolina. You have to understand that heaven is your real reality. What happens is that we have all of these distractions that come from this world. This world comes to suck the life out of you. This world comes to suck your drive and 'your seek' for God out of you. You have to refocus your focus. The Bible says in Proverbs 29:18 that "Where there is no vision, the people perish". That verse means you cast off restraint and lose hope because you don't see where you should be going.

Here is Jesus telling the disciples to refocus. He wanted them to look at Him. Stop looking at your bank account. Stop looking at your job. Your job is a resource and not your source. Resources and sources are two different things. God is your source. What has happened is we've been treating Pharaoh like he is our source. That's why he keeps telling us to make those bricks. He knows that when he tells you to make those bricks, you have your mind on the money, so he keeps telling you to put the bricks out. All the while, you're toiling in the field making bricks, forgetting your Kingdom focus. Jesus knew what He was talking about. The Bible says in verse 24 that "No one can serve two masters, for either he will hate the one and love the other." I'm saying to you that you must begin to think radically. You

219

must begin to challenge what this world and society has told you are the norms. The norm in the Kingdom of God is abnormal in the world. We have been going along and walking in agreement with the world. We have the same goals they have, when in essence, they should be looking to us and asking us what our goals are. We are walking too close with this world. We are all tied up in this world. Now don't get me wrong. I understand that you have to work and take care of your business. But what I'm saying to you is that you have to make sure that your first and foremost focus is what Jesus said in verse 33. We have to seek the Kingdom of God before anything else. Let 'your seek' for the Kingdom of God have precedence over everything else. What is happened is that Jesus has become recreational. Church has become recreational because 'our seek' is on other things. What are you gonna do if God cuts off your resource? You'll be in church every Sunday. You will be standing outside the church asking for extra services. Why do you have to wait for all hell to break loose for you to start seeking after the Kingdom? In reality, you don't want the Kingdom. You just want the benefits of the Kingdom. I can't have the benefits from a job unless I work that job. I can't go in there talking about being covered by insurance with the transit authority if I don't work for the transit authority. They won't find my name in the system. If I don't work for them, they don't cover me. If you work for the Kingdom, God covers you.

We need to store up heavenly things. You have to shift your focus. You have to begin to pray more. You have to begin to fast more. Do you know why some stuff won't break off of you? It's because you won't fast. You won't turn the hellivision off long enough to hear God. You can't hear God because you're listening to the theme from CSI. I'm not saying don't watch television, I'm saying do all things in moderation. Where is your seek? 'Your seek' has been lost because you killed it with the things of this world. You have put yourself to sleep, and when you come to church we have to revive and resuscitate you. You have to want to live. You have to seek God. It's not about this world. We have to wear this world loosely instead of carrying it all on our backs.

I heard a story about a man who told his wife to empty out his bank account and put everything he had in the coffin with him when he died. So the preacher that was doing the eulogy told him to give him the money and the he would write a check and let him know when it hit the bank. Why are we trying to take all of this stuff with us? You are not taking any of it with you when you leave here. Wouldn't it be nice if we got on our faces and sought the Lord before we looked in the classified section for a job? That's order. Instead we walk around frustrated because we can't find jobs. We go and knock on doors and fill out applications and wonder why nobody has called. Nobody has called because you didn't call Jesus yet. Seek ye first the Kingdom. Stop trying to seek after job applications. Seek God first. I'm telling you how you're going to get stuff in alignment. Don't seek what you think is right. Seek what God thinks is right.

Here's what verse 33 says in The Message Bible: "Steep your life in God-reality, God-initiative, God-provisions. Don't worry about missing out. You'll find all your everyday human concerns will be met." If you seek God first... I would to God that we would pray every morning before we went to work. I know you have to go to work early, but if you can jump out of bed for Pharaoh, why can't you roll out of bed for Jesus? I'm not understanding that. Matthew 6:21 tells us: "For where your treasure is, there will your heart be also." Where our heart is, that's where our treasure is. I'm not talking about tithes and offerings. Let's just talk about where your focus is. You can't break free because you have the wrong focus. You're not just bound by your situation - your heart is in that situation. When you were supposed to be seeking after God, you let something else fill that void. I've been guilty. I've done that. And every day I'm fighting against everything that wants to attach itself to me. I'm fighting against everything that wants to steal my prayer life, everything that wants to steal my fasting life, and everything that wants to get in the way of me reading the Word. This is where I have to get concentrated. I can't make it out here without the Word. Neither can you. Stop thinking you're gonna quit on your own. You don't have enough strength to quit on your own. If you could, you would've done it already.

Jesus took them up into a mountain, which denoted a going up, an ascended thinking, and a leaving of some people and things behind at ground level so that they could get to where God was. Sometimes you have to get away from folks. Reality is that you cannot walk with everybody and be saved. The enemy of your soul doesn't like you. He will send every kind of distraction including friends and loved ones to come to try to hinder you and keep you walking upright before the Lord. Jesus says that we are supposed to seek the Kingdom of God and His righteousness first and that all the other things will be added. When Jesus talks about the Kingdom, what He's telling us is that He

223

wants us to stop trying to get power with our boss and understand that He has given us a position in His kingdom that has power. He's saying, "I want you to understand that the Kingdom comes with kingdom authority and kingdom power." You can't get your eyes fixed on that if you're hanging out with the wrong crowd of folks.

I want to look at Colossians 3:1 - "If then you have been raised with Christ, seek the things that are above, where Christ is, seated at the right hand of God." I love the fact that when Paul is writing this, he says "if". Everybody that is claiming salvation isn't saved. They are not saved. I'm sick of this stuff and how we try to come up in church and tell people that they are saved. Just because you came to the altar and prayer doesn't make you saved. Jesus said, "Go your way and sin no more." Paul said IF you are risen with Christ. That means that it's conditional. You are not getting any benefits without meeting the conditions. You aren't understanding why God isn't hearing, but it's because you haven't put those cigarettes down. You're still sipping on the side and still saying that you're saved. You are not saved. I would rather you get mad at me today and roll your eyes and suck your teeth and get right with God and go to heaven than to still be in your mess thinking that you're saved and die and go to hell. You need to come to terms with it. Figure out if you are really saved. You're not saved if you're still cussing. How can you seek those things which are above if your flesh is driving you to those things that are earthly? This is why Jesus had to take them into the mountain. He knew that the temptation for their jobs was still down there in the valley. He knew that their loved ones were still down there in the valley. Have you ever gone in the room and tried to pray and had a knock at the door? That's rough. I could be in the Spirit snotting and crying and if someone would interrupt my prayer it would not be pretty at all. I will jump out of the Spirit because of someone being in the way of my seeking the Kingdom of God. I want us to stir up some devils. You are going to have to leave some people in the background. Leave them where they are because we have to deal with putting Jesus first.

Let's look at Psalm 37. For those of you who are Bible scholars, this is a cross-reference to what we read in Matthew 6:33. Why is this verse we are getting ready to read a cross-reference? Psalm 37:21-25 says:

"The wicked borrows but does not pay back, but the righteous is generous and gives; for those blessed by the Lord[c] shall inherit the land, but those cursed by him shall be cut off. The steps of a man are established by the Lord, when he delights in his way; though he fall, he shall not be cast headlong, for the Lord upholds his hand. I have been young, and now am old, yet I have not seen the righteous forsaken or his children begging for bread."

Let me encourage you for a quick second. You might be struggling, you might be having a hard time, you might be having problems, but don't stay there. You have to get up from where you are. If you are going to walk in the blessings of God, you have to get up from where you are. What messes us up is that we get discouraged because we fall and then we start wallowing. You can't get up to the mountain and wallow at the same time. It's impossible. You cannot be two places at one time. You are one person. Loose here talking about out-of-body experiences.

I love the fact that a lot of us quote this Scripture but do not live this. People quote this and aren't even righteous. Like I said to you, this is a cross-reference for Matthew 6:33, so what is this telling me? If I'm not a kingdom seeker, then I'm not righteous. If I'm not seeking the Kingdom, I'm just a churchgoer. I'm just a religious person. I'm not a kingdom seeker. Being here does not make me a part of the Kingdom. Remember that Paul said IF you be risen. Let's deal with "if". What's working on your "if"? What's keeping you from being risen with Christ? What habit? What mentality? What proclivities? What things are you dealing with that are keeping you bound and keeping you from seeking the Kingdom? What is it? If I seek the Kingdom, and if I put all of my priorities in place... If I stop trying to establish myself and allow God to establish me, then I can say that "I have been young and now I'm old, yet have I not seen the righteous forsaken nor His seed begging bread." You have to live by faith before you can claim the Scripture. You are still claiming that your job is your source. Stop trying to claim the Scripture. You have not even learned to believe God. What if God told you to take off your job for the next thirty days and just seek Me? We would need a word of confirmation. You know it's true. You would not be looking for just one confirmation, either. You would want more than one confirmation because you would think it wasn't God. You would be quoting the bible talking about how if you don't work you don't eat and you would think it wasn't God. That's our problem - we have our minds on eating. We are not missing any meals. We could stand a fast. We won't die if we miss a couple of meals. This tells me that we have been seeking

IHOP. We've been seeking Olive Garden. We have been seeking seafood. I'm guilty.

Seek ye first the Kingdom of God. Stop looking for all this other stuff and start looking for Jesus. What would you do if you lost your job today other than have a fit? How would you respond? We might say "Thank You Jesus" after we got ourselves together, but we would scream and holler first. We would be ready to tell the boss off. Seek ye first the Kingdom. We need to get to the place where we are praying without ceasing. Nothing should come upon the children of God unaware. Get in a place of seeing. There is a place of hearing in the Spirit, but when you are not in prayer you can't see and you can't hear. Then when stuff happens we cry out to God asking Him what in the world is going on. You mean to tell me that all this stuff is going on and there isn't a prophet in the house? Is this the church of the living God? If we would seek the Kingdom, the President and everybody else would be seeking after us. You know why? Because there would be a word in our mouths. That means that you are not going to be bought by anybody. They can keep their offering and you will still preach what God says.

If I have to get out there and panhandle, I am going to preach what Jesus said. I'm not about to be stuck. We let everything control us when God is looking for a people who will just slap go out of their mind and obey Him. It should be that when the world sees you, you disturb them. When you sit next to a sinner it should disturb them. Instead, they are cozy sitting next to us. They are so comfortable. Whose life is being disturbed because of the Holy Ghost in you? That's how we know we're living something. But the fact of the matter is that folks walk up to us and curse and we laugh it off thinking it's cute and funny. What? No. You are in the Kingdom. You need to bring some correction. You need to tell people not to speak that language in your holy ears. You have to have a kingdom mindset. If you want God to meet your needs and if you want to be able to stop struggling, this right here is the answer to your struggle. How can I stop struggling? Seek the Kingdom. Seek the King and His kingdom. Don't just look for the benefits package. Look for the King.

Let's go to Mark 10:17-31.

"And as he was setting out on his journey, a man ran up and knelt before him and asked him, "Good Teacher, what must I do to inherit eternal life? And Jesus said to him, "Why do you call me good? No one is good except God alone. You know the commandments: 'Do not murder, Do not commit adultery, Do not steal, Do not bear false witness, Do not defraud, Honor your father and mother. And he said to him, "Teacher, all these I have kept from my youth. And Jesus, looking at him, loved him, and said to him, "You lack one thing: go, sell all that you have and give to the poor, and you will have treasure in heaven; and come, follow me. Disheartened by the saying, he went away sorrowful, for he had great possessions.

And Jesus looked around and said to his disciples, "How difficult it will be for those who have wealth to enter the kingdom of God! And the disciples were amazed at his words. But Jesus said to them again, "Children, how difficult it is [b] to enter the kingdom of God! It is easier for a camel to go through the eye of a needle than for a rich person to enter the kingdom of God. And they were exceedingly astonished, and said to him, "Then who can be saved? Jesus looked at them and said, "With man it is impossible, but not with God. For all things are possible with God. Peter began to say to him, "See, we have left everything and followed you." Jesus said, "Truly, I say to you, there is no one who has left house or brothers or sisters or mother or father or children or lands, for my sake and for the Gospel, who will not receive a hundredfold now in this time, houses and brothers and sisters and mothers and children and lands, with persecutions, and in the age to come eternal life. But many who are first will be last, and the last first."

In this passage, Jesus has an encounter with the young rich man. He deals with him because he is zealous and he's a seeker, but he's seeking after the wrong thing. Now, the Bible tells us in Ecclesiastes 10:19 that money answers all things, so don't get it twisted. I'm not saying anything negative about money. What I am saying is that you need to be mindful of your focus. I'm saying that if Jesus told you to give it all up today (not tomorrow), what would your decision be? How would you respond? Are you so attached to your money that you're like this young man? Do you feel like because you go to church and pray and ready your word every now and then, you're okay? You do all those things that you think are going to get you closer to God, but He doesn't really have your heart. How do I know? Because as soon as He puts His hand in your treasure, we have a problem. As soon as He burns our barley fields, we have a problem. Why? Because He never had it in the first place. This is not the hour to be a shabby Christian. Honestly, I can't even call you a shabby Christian because that's an oxymoron. Those two words don't even go together. You aren't a shabby believer. You are unsaved. You have to come to terms with your own actions, with your own mindsets, and with whatever it is that is keeping you from seeking the King and the Kingdom. Stop looking for His benefits and look for Him. Look for Him.

When you go to Luke 12:22-34 it's the same story as in Matthew 6: "And he said to his disciples, "Therefore I tell you, do not be anxious about your life, what you will eat, nor about your body, what you will put on. For life is more than food, and the body more than clothing. Consider the ravens: they neither sow nor reap, they have neither storehouse nor barn, and yet God feeds them. Of how much more value are you than the birds! And which of you by being anxious can add a single hour to his span of life? If then you are not able to do as small a thing as that, why are you anxious about the rest? Consider the lilies, how they grow: they neither toil nor spin, yet I tell you, even Solomon in all his glory was not arrayed like one of these. But if God so clothes the grass, which is alive in the field today, and tomorrow is thrown into the oven, how much more will he clothe you, O you of little faith! And do not seek what you are to eat and what you are to drink, nor be worried. For all the nations of the world seek after these things, and your Father knows that you need them. Instead, seek his kingdom, and these things will be added to you. Fear not, little flock, for it is your Father's good pleasure to give you the kingdom. Sell your possessions, and give to the needy. Provide yourselves with moneybags that do not grow old, with a treasure in the heavens that does not fail, where no thief approaches and no moth destroys. For where your treasure is, there will your heart be also."

One of the things you have to realize is that it is impossible to have Pharaoh's heart and God's heart at the same time. You can't do it. My goddaughter was telling me that she was working for a pastor and the pastor had a daycare center. The pastor was offering her a better job with better pay working in the office of the daycare center. In order for her to do that, he told her that she couldn't have the job unless she left her church. The devil is a liar. What kind of foolishness is that? The girl is saved and loves the Lord. Shouldn't that be the only prerequisite right there? But because he is trying to get control, really this shows us that people are not really kingdom seekers. We're looking for numbers. We're trying to impress man. We're trying to make man happy - later for man. Thank God for man (in general), but later for man. You don't have time to please anybody but God. And if that makes your family mad, oh well. Are you radical like that to the point that you make your family mad having to stand for Jesus? Now you know the truth, the whole truth, and the whole truth is that the moment we know that we are going to experience opposition we back down. This is especially true when it comes to our parents. We feel like we can't say certain things to our parents. No. God's standard is God's standard. You have to be willing to hold up God's standard no matter what.

1 Timothy 4:8 (King James Version) states: "For bodily exercise profiteth little: but godliness is profitable unto all things, having promise of the life that now is, and of that which is to come." A lot of times people say, "Well you don't know if you're going to die today." I beg to differ. If you are in the presence of God, God said that He would do NOTHING except He first reveal it to His servants the prophets (Amos 3:7). God doesn't move outside of His Word. If you are in the dark, you just need to turn the light on. If you didn't know, that means you didn't go far enough. You have to get up in the mountain. Here he's saying that not only do you have a promise of the life to come, but that the devil is not going to come and be able to suck you out of the life you have now. You're not going to die before your time. Has anybody ever come against generational curses in your family? That's good news right here in the Word. We not only have a

promise of the life that is to come. God promises to order our steps every day of our life. We can walk in revelation knowing what the will of the Lord is. The Bible says that we should be able to know what the will of the Lord is. God's will is not for you to walk in darkness. He wants you to know. He doesn't want anything springing up on you. But when we don't go far enough in Him that causes problems. That causes us to live in darkness. That causes us to be caught off guard. Aren't you tired of being caught off guard? Miss Cleo should not be in the know before a man of God or a woman of God. Loose here. That is not God. Psychics and lying spirits shouldn't have all the information. The devil knows what he is going to do, so that is not a Word from God. You must refocus and get your head in the game if you're going to win.

Chapter Eleven

For The Men: Just Be A Man

As I begin this section. I do so with caution. While having every intention to speak with candor and love, there is the realization that at times it is difficult for men to receive a message from women without being offended by her audacity and fervor. These words will cut. So, for my brothers who dare to proceed to read this chapter, do begin reading with ears attentive to this truth with the love that is intended, as well as keeping your heart open to the chastening of the Lord.

No one is perfect. Not one man or one woman. This chapter is no indictment against men. It is a clarion call for the brotherhood to come back into alignment with what has been ordained at creation. Most men, especially those with any form of religious background or biblical knowledge, are familiar with the fact that the man is the "head" of the woman. That's the no-brainer. The hardship follows when those who have been called to be the head, have lost their place and struggle to regain it. Most women are in your corner and want a strong leading man. However, it is no secret that the girls are not the only ones who need to "Get a Grip!" This chapter is a prayerful attempt to push the man back to the front of the line: Albeit with a swift kick. As you read, let love be heard, felt and the words received so that you too, man can encourage others and say "Boy, Get a Grip!"

2 Samuel 10 1-19

"After this the king of the Ammonites died, and Hanun his son reigned in his place. And David said, "I will deal loyally with Hanun the son of Nahash, as his father dealt loyally with me." So David sent by his servants to console him concerning his father. And David's servants came into the land of the Ammonites. But the princes of the Ammonites said to Hanun their lord, "Do you think, because David has sent comforters to you, that he is honoring your father? Has not David sent his servants to you to search the city and to spy it out and to overthrow it? So Hanun took David's servants and shaved off half the beard of each and cut off their garments in the middle, at their hips, and sent them away. When it was told David, he sent to meet them, for the men were greatly ashamed. And the king said, "Remain at Jericho until your beards have grown and then return. When the Ammonites saw that they had become a stench to David, the Ammonites sent and hired the Syrians of Beth-rehob, and the Syrians of Zobah, 20,000-foot soldiers, and the king of Maacah with 1,000 men, and the men of Tob, 12,000 men. And when David heard of it, he sent Joab and all the host of the mighty men. And the Ammonites came out and drew up in battle array at the entrance of the gate, and the Syrians of Zobah and of Rehob and the men of Tob and Maacah were by themselves in the open country. When Joab saw that the battle was set against him both in front and in the rear, he chose some of the best men of Israel and arrayed them against the Syrians. The rest of his men he put in the charge of Abishai his brother, and he arrayed them against the Ammonites. And he said, "If the Syrians are too strong for me, then you shall help me, but if the Ammonites are too strong for you, then I will come and help you. Be of good courage, and let us be courageous for our people, and for the cities of our God, and may the Lord do what seems good to him."

So Joab and the people who were with him drew near to battle against the Syrians, and they fled before him. And when the Ammonites saw that the Syrians fled, they likewise fled before Abishai and entered the city. Then Joab returned from fighting against the Ammonites and came to Jerusalem. But when the Syrians saw that they had been defeated by Israel, they gathered themselves together. And Hadadezer sent and brought out the Syrians who were beyond the Euphrates. They came to Helam, with Shobach the commander of the army of Hadadezer at their head. And when it was told David, he gathered all Israel together and crossed the Jordan and came to Helam. The Syrians arrayed themselves against David and fought with him. And the Syrians fled before Israel, and David killed of the Syrians the men of 700 chariots, and 40,000 horsemen, and wounded Shobach the commander of their army, so that he died there.

And when all the kings who were servants of Hadadezer saw that they had been defeated by Israel, they made peace with Israel and became subject to them. So the Syrians were afraid to save the Ammonites anymore."

There are a couple of things that I want to go back through concerning this text. The first thing is that while you are in the midst of a battle, you need to be careful of who is whispering in your ear. You need to be mindful. Here is a king who was placed in authority after his father died and David meant him good. He missed an opportunity to remain at peace with someone his father had developed relationship with. He knew from the track record that David was at peace with his father. David sent peaceful words to the king's son after the king died. Here he was listening to the wrong people instead of him really listening to what David was saying. When you are in the midst of a battle and a fight for your life, you have to be careful about who is talking to you.

This applies to all of us. We come together and a word is delivered, and as soon as the word is delivered, here comes the enemy trying to whisper in our ears. I know it's right. The enemy tries to have us panicking and thinking about stuff that isn't even happening. Have you ever thought that something was going on that really wasn't going on, and then you end up messing yourself up because you talked yourself into some nonsense? That has happened to me. This mind right here, if you don't get this mind right (especially when you're in the midst of a fight) you'll be messed up. Your thoughts are already off anyway when you are going through, so you don't need to be talking yourself out of anything. You have to be careful of who is talking in your ear. Don't you let the devil come and tell you anything. Instead of this king exercised wisdom, he like a dummy listened to them and instigated a fight against Israel. Help us Jesus. Sometimes we end up fighting the people God intended to be our friends instead of seeing that God had meant them to be on our side. There's nothing worse than fighting a friend. Nothing is worse than that. Be careful who is whispering in your ear.

Verse four says, "So Hanun took David's servants and shaved off half the beard of each and cut off their garments in the middle, at their hips, and sent them away." The Lord began to speak to me and let me know that we lost some things as we started going through our battles. Just as quick as God blessed us, poured into us, anointed us, and refreshed our spirits, we entered right back into another battle and the enemy tricked us. This happens between one Sunday and the next Sunday. The enemy came in and tried to strip us and make us ashamed. He wanted us to feel like God wasn't about to do it and that we weren't really about to break through. By them getting their beards shaved off and their clothes cut in half, the enemy was doing the same thing. He was uncovering them so that other people could see their shame. He wants to uncover us so that everybody can see what we are going through. The enemy tries to do stuff to try to make us feel bad and to make us feel like everybody is looking at us and judging what we are going through. The enemy does this right after we get our victory. We get our victory one minute and the next minute we find ourselves right back in the middle of another test.

Verse five says that they were greatly ashamed, but I like verse six. It says, "When the Ammonites saw that they had become a stench to David, the Ammonites sent and hired the Syrians of Beth-rehob." The devil thinks he's slick. He just swears that he's slick. He picked a fight and didn't know who he was messing with. He's nothing but a big bully who is always nagging and talking smack but then when you get in the fight he has to go get some demons to help him. These brothers couldn't even fight the fight they started. They started the fight but the verse says that they hired the Syrians. Do you know what this tells me? It tells me that the enemy is all bark and no bite. Have you ever seen a big dog sitting in the yard doing a whole lot of barking? You can throw him a piece of chicken or something and he'll be your friend. All bark and no bite. There's nothing worse than listening to a dog who has a fierce bark but when you look at him in his mouth he has no teeth. The most he can do is gum you. I'm not telling you that the enemy has no authority and power, but I want you to understand that he knows that this fight is fixed. You are the one who has to realize and know that this fight is fixed. I don't care what else breaks down, burns down, falls down, or falls apart. God has my back. This is what we have to know. You cannot panic. David did not panic when he say his enemy coming. David was ready for the fight.

What he did was go to get his mighty men. That's what I like. God is not gonna put any wimpy men on the front line. When it comes to the brothers, just be a man. When the Scriptures talk about being a man, they are talking about maturity. We aren't talking about gender - gender has nothing to do with it. Women, we need to be mature. Men, you need to be mature too. Verse nine says, "When Joab saw that the battle was set against him both in front and in the rear, he chose some of the best men of Israel and arrayed them against the Syrians." Let me tell you something: This verse is prophetic. There are things the enemy is sending to try to fight your future. There are also things from your past he sends to try to fight you. The reason why he wants to hinder you is that he doesn't want you to get to what God has for you in your future. He doesn't even want you to lay your eyes on it. He doesn't want you to even get a picture of it in your spirit. There will always be stuff behind you that the enemy will always try to send up. You have already gotten free and are headed to your destiny, and here comes the past trying to knock on your door.

We have to remember that we are in the midst of a fight for our very life. We are fighting for our spiritual life. We aren't just fighting for ourselves. Remember the story of Hezekiah (2 Kings 20) and how when he received the word that he was going to die, he turned his face to the wall. God had already spoken and said that there was going to be a curse to come upon him. Hezekiah turned his face to the wall and God gave him fifteen more years, and then the prophet came back and told him that those things would not come upon him but that they would come upon his sons. Hezekiah thought that was a good thing because he felt like it meant that he wouldn't have any trouble. Dummy. Dumb king. That's why we have to be men in the Spirit. We have to listen to what God is saying. We have to fight the past that is trying to come back upon us and we have to fight for our future. Why? Because if I don't fight for my future, the same curse that was hindering me and trying to come against me will try to come against my seed. Hezekiah didn't care about his seed. He only cared about himself. That's a sad repertoire for a father. That's a sad king and a sad man.

That's not the will of God. God does not want us as women and men of God to just be concerned about ourselves. We have to be concerned about our future.

Let's go over to 1 Corinthians 16:13 which says, "Be watchful, stand firm in the faith, act like men, be strong." Do you know what that means? It means stop acting like a sissy. Stop whining. Stop complaining. That's for all of us. Paul was talking to the whole church. He was talking to the men and the women. Stop whining and complaining. Stop acting like you're in this thing by yourself. Hold on to what God has given you. Hold on to what God has spoken to you. Hold on to what God did for you last week. We ought to be coming to church tearing up some chairs just because the enemy had the audacity to try us. Do you want to fight or not? It's too late to try to decide. Stop being a sissy. Act manly. Stop whining and crying and snotting. Stop asking why. Why not? It's all right that you have to deal with whatever you have to deal with. Man up. Grow up. Let us take these things that God has placed in our hand and let's fight like men. Paul is saying to act manly. For the men, he's saying to be a husband. Be strong. I know sometimes it's hard to be strong when you have everything you can think of coming against you and you're ready to go off. Thank God for the Holy Ghost because we would have said some choice words and done some things. Thank God for the Holy Ghost! Man up. Wake up. You cannot fall asleep on this watch. I don't care how tired or aggravated you might be. I don't care how your body is going through. I don't care how your mind is going through. I don't care who is whispering in your ear. Watch! Paul told us to watch and stand firm. That's a fighting position.

This is a true story, I promise. We came to the church one night and it was dark outside. We came inside and I was back there in the youth church. He came to the door in the back and he stuck his head out the door. For some reason, he just felt led to go to the door. I heard him talking to someone and asking if he could help him. When he said that, something in me rose up because it didn't feel right. I picked up a pole and went to the door. I was not playing. Don't be coming up on God's property thinking you're about to do something. My son said that he came outside and there was a man standing outside by the van. I bet that spirit was telling him to go ahead. He had better be glad he didn't go ahead, because he would have had a pole sticking out of his head, in Jesus' name. I ain't playing with the devil. We would have claimed his deliverance right there. I am not playing with the devil. Why are you playing? Be a man. When you start saying that you are going to take territory for the Lord, the enemy is going to try you. He is going to say, "Are you really serious? Let's see if you're really serious." If you're not up for a fight, you may as well take your seat now and stay seated. We are either going to stand up and be in the fight knowing that the fight is fixed or we are going to sit down. The enemy will try to snatch your prayer life, your fasting, your bible time, your dedication, and your mind. You have to watch and you have to stand firm in your faith. You have to man up. You have to be a man in the Spirit. You have to be mature in the Spirit. I'm not going to send my kids to go fight any battles for me. David called for the mighty men. That means that you could trust them. They had a spirit like Peter. Jesus had to tell Peter to back up because he was just ready to kill everybody, and there is a time for that. I'm trying to tell you that if that man would have walked up in the church... Here's the thing: There is something in your spirit when you know that things just aren't right. I just heard him hollering out the door "Can I help you?" He didn't raise his voice, but in my spirit I felt like something wasn't right so I walked towards the door and I grabbed that stick. This ain't no time to be scared. I don't care if it's dark outside. You can use that in the spirit as well. I don't care how dark it is in the spirit - you have to be ready to go for it and fight. The devil ain't playing and I ain't playing. But like I said, the devil is all bark and no bite. He has to go get his cohorts to help him fight.

The enemy comes to try to get us off track and distracted. The enemy comes to try to wear us out. One thing, after the other thing, after the other thing, after the other thing. When we get worn out, we make dumb choices, kind of like the king. You have to take the time to get on your face to hear from God. Stay in His Word. How can you watch if you have no Word in you? What are you watching for? What alarms are going to go off if you're not connected to the vine?

Let's look at Colossians 2:6-10 & 15 (King James Version).

"As ye have therefore received Christ Jesus the Lord, so walk ye in him: Rooted and built up in him, and stablished in the faith, as ye have been taught, abounding therein with thanksgiving. Beware lest any man spoil you through philosophy and vain deceit, after the tradition of men, after the rudiments of the world, and not after Christ. For in him dwelleth all the fulness of the Godhead bodily. And ye are complete in him, which is the head of all principality and power: And having spoiled principalities and powers, he made a shew of them openly, triumphing over them in it."

Everything we need is already in Jesus. We are complete in Him. My authority comes through Him. The power that I have in God comes through Jesus. We have to be in the place of understanding that when we are fighting a fight, it's not in us anyway. For a long time people would come to me and prophesy and say, "You know it's not you, right?" I would always wonder why they said that to me because I already knew that. The Lord said to me, "No, I need you to understand that though you may be smart and gifted, I have something you ain't have. There is something you have to get that you can only get through me. There is something that I'm going to do through you that no matter how much you study, no matter how much you pray, you're gonna have to just lean back on Me and let me flow through you." It's the same thing when we are fighting battles. I love to read, but even all of that knowledge is no good unless God moves and puts His spirit behind that thing. You have to understand that everything we need is in Christ Jesus. He has given us power over all principalities and powers because He has the power. It's not because we prayed. That's really what my point is. You're not powerful because you fasted.

You're not powerful because you prayed. You're not powerful because you read your Bible from Genesis to Revelation. You're powerful because Jesus did the work. It's as simple as that. If we don't get that, we are all back on works. If my fasting and praying was all I needed to have power and authority over the devil, then I don't have to rely on Jesus. I can just work my way to a place of power. God wants you to know that He needs you to just rely on Him and rest in His authority. Rest on everything that was done on Calvary for you. That gives me courage because what if I'm tired? What if I only read a couple of verses that day? That has nothing to do with it! It's on God. It's on His back. He has to do the work. Hallelujah!

Verse fifteen says: "And having spoiled principalities and powers, he made a show of them openly, triumphing over them in it." Isn't that something? Going back to 2 Samuel where we see that the enemy made fun of David and his men and embarrassed them in front of everybody... and here comes Jesus. We get to skip testaments and get on over here in the New Testament where we see that Jesus made an open show of the enemy. What he did was basically the same thing that happened to David's men. He stripped the enemy naked in front of everybody for all principalities and all powers to see that He had all power and authority over the enemy. So in essence, what happened is that the devil went running with his booty hanging out. That's what happened. If you study, you will see that this is what happened. He made an open show of the enemy. We have to understand the power that's in Jesus. Thank God that He lives on the inside of us. I'm glad that it's not relying on what I can and cannot do. It's all about what Jesus can do through me if I just make myself available and get the mindset to just be a man. Just get the mindset. If I think like a man, then I can act like a man. I'm not talking about being off gender-wise. This has nothing to do with gender. I'm talking about in the Spirit. Man up in the Spirit.

There reason we have to do this is because there is so much we are fighting for. There is so much that is at stake. We're talking about our past trying to run up on us, and the enemy trying to steal our future. There is so much we are fighting for right now. The enemy wants to come to try and wreck our homes. He wants to wreck our children. He wants to wreck our personal destinies. When he realized that we aren't going to go anywhere, he looks for the next thing to hit us with. You have to be a man in the Spirit. You have to be tenacious. You have to grab a hold of God and not accept anything but what God's Word says.

I know I sound like a broken record but you have to get this. The evidence of whether or not you get it is that if you get it, your house will change accordingly. I believe that if we just believe God like we're a bunch of crazy folks... Things will happen when we start really believing the Word. You will not be able to make it in this life and do the things that God said you would be able to do unless you go crazy. You're gonna have to just be a little crazy. Just a touch.

I have too much I'm fighting for. I'm tired of the devil. I hate him. I'm tired of him crossing the line. When are you gonna get mad at the devil for crossing the line? We need to start jacking him on the left and on the right. Do you remember how people would try to bully you in school? That's how I turned into a bully. I got tired of bullied and became a terror in my own right. I got tired of people pushing me around. That's that "snapping" in the Holy Ghost. Can we snap just one more time in the Holy Ghost? We have to really get serious about this thing. Until you get mad and tired, you will keep taking things the enemy dishes out to you. Be a man about it. Grow up. It is time to put up or shut up. If you don't have the goods, go get someone who does. I don't have time to be playing games. Any time I hear anybody say anything about just trusting God, I just go off in my spirit. I'm serious.

I am waiting for Him to manifest what He said He's going to do. I'm going to keep saying it until I see it. When I get it, everybody will know that I have it because I will be rolling in the floor and giving God glory. Why? Because I know that He is a God of His Word. He is not a man that He should lie (Numbers 23:19). I want your faith to be charged. I want you to be mad at the devil. I want you to be a man and get out there and kick some devil hiney. That's what I want to see you do. Be a bulldog about it. Meet that devil on the playground after school. I don't' have to go get anybody but my big brother Jesus. I can't fight without Him.

1 Corinthians 9:26 (KJV) says, " I therefore so run, not as uncertainly; so fight I, not as one that beateth the air." The devil will try to make you feel like you aren't getting any victory but the devil is a liar. I am gaining some ground. I'm not just beating the air. I might feel tired. I might feel like I'm gaining anything, but I'm so glad that victory isn't a feeling. Victory is a reality, and it's my reality. It's your reality. You have to know that it is your reality. I'm going to tell you something: Talking talk picks a fight. If you're going to talk like this, you'd better put your gloves on. Put your sneakers on. You are going

to have to man up if you're gonna talk the talk. If you believe God and trust God, then you have to stand on that word.

Let's go to 1 Timothy 6:12 (KJV).

"Fight the good fight of faith, lay hold on eternal life, whereunto thou art also called, and hast professed a good profession before many witnesses."

You can't just say one thing and do another. Really what Paul is telling Timothy in this verse is that whatever he says is what he needs to do. We can't just talk about it but we really need to be about it. I had to break these words down.

The first word "fight" comes from the Greek word "agónizomai" which is the same word for "agonize" or "agony". This means to wrestle and persevere in the midst of opposition and temptation; to make every effort to obtain a goal; to wrestle for a prize; to suffer special pain and toil. It implies hindrances.

The word "good" is from the Greek word "kalos" which means valuable, fair or worthy; or something that is beneficial.

253

You have one kind of fight in the beginning, but after the word "good" there is another kind of fight. This word "fight" comes from the same root "agon" which means to force; violence, strife or contention; a contest for mastery; a struggle or the struggle of the Christian life; to carry away with violence; to get the spoil

I'm going to give you the translation of that verse based on those words. It means to fight, wrestle and agonize, endure the special pains and toil, and overcome every hindrance as you endure this worthy, valuable and beneficial fight that will be good to you in the end; for you will violently and forcefully struggle to contend so that you will carry away violently the spoil of the battle. You're not going to just get anything from the enemy. You will have to take it violently. Matthew 11:12-14 says that the kingdom of heaven suffers violence and the violent take it by force. You are not going to get anything being passive. Now you can whisper a prayer but there needs to be some power behind that whisper. You are going to have to get down and get dirty. That means you will have to get some dirt underneath your fingernails. Your clothes are going to get jacked up. You may as well pull your hair back, put some Vaseline on, take your earrings off and get ready. Brothers, you just put your sneakers on and be ready to go. Although it may not feel like it right now, it will be worth the fight when you are done. When you are finished, you will understand what all of it was for and you will be glad that you stayed in the fight and didn't give up. You will be glad that you endured to the end.

If you're going to carry away spoils, that means that you will have to plunder your enemy. You have to go into his territory and take what he has taken that he has no right to have. There are things that the enemy has snatched that he has no right to have. He has no right to our children. John 10:10 (KJV) says that "The thief cometh not, but for to steal, and to kill, and to destroy: I am come that they might have life, and that they might have it more abundantly." We're not talking about the abundance of houses, cars and money. That right there is frivolous. We need a car, we need a house, and we need some money. God already knows what we need, so why are you tripping about a house and a car? Let's get to the weightier matters. Let's go after the souls of men. Paul talks in the book of Jude about snatching some out of the fire and hating even the garment that has been spotted by the flesh. Who will want to go in and fight the devil for some souls?

That's where the battle is. Who wants to get down and dirty and fast and pray? Who wants to travail and pray until we see souls come in from darkness to the light? That's where the battle is, because the devil wants the souls of men. The Bible says in Psalm 2:8 that God will give us the heathen for our inheritance. If God left you something, you have to want it. If you don't state a claim to your inheritance, you will never receive it. All souls belong to God. God already put the tools in our hands. You have everything you need to make the battle yours, but you have to do something about it. You have to have a mindset that you are not giving up or letting go. You can't give up on prayer just because you have a hard time praying one day. The devil is a liar. You have to persevere. That's what this verse is saying in 1 Timothy 6:12. You have to persevere and press through because the god of this world doesn't like you. He can't stand you. He doesn't want you to obtain your goals. He doesn't want you to get the victory. He wants you to give up. I'm thanking God that He will raise up some men that will fight for our children. We will follow these men as they fight for our children. Women, we will keep praying that God will put the men where they should be. That's the will of God. Men, we are going to love you, encourage you, and speak life to you because we want to follow you. We want to follow you as you follow Christ. That's the will of God. Don't take this the wrong way - it's encouraging. It is the will of God that we act like men. Just be a man. Just be. If you don't know how to be a man, get in the Word and let it speak to you about how to be a man.

Chapter Twelve

For Your Relationships: How We Fight

Sometimes in dealing with relationships, when we get angry, the first thing we do is cut everybody off and go off to our little corners. We stop talking. We estrange ourselves from everybody. Just to recap from last week, we talked about what it means to communicate and the different communication. We have verbal and nonverbal communication. We communicate with our gestures and facial expressions. We communicate with our language. We send messages even when we are saying that we are okay and really our body language tells something altogether different. We talked about the biblical foundation for marriage and how the Bible says that it is not good for man to be alone (Genesis 2:18). We talked about how the two shall be come one flesh (Genesis 2:24) physically, emotionally and spiritually. We need to be able to be in the state where it okay for us to be naked (not just without clothes) with our mate. When we enter into covenant, covenant is a binding agreement. We have to learn how to persevere through our covenant. We are too quick to be ready to divorce one another, and we need to learn how to work through stuff and work it out.

We are beginning with the cycle of disaffection. What gets us started? There is a cycle that we begin in. Whenever you start talking about being angry and offended, you get started in a cycle.

We are going to look at Ecclesiastes 9:9: "Live joyfully with the wife whom thou lovest all the days of the life of thy vanity, which he hath given thee under the sun, all the days of thy vanity: for that is thy portion in this life, and in thy labour which thou takest under the sun." The English Standard Version states: "Enjoy life with the wife whom you love, all the days of your vain life that he has given you under the sun, because that is your portion in life and in your toil at which you toil under the sun." We are talking about the fact that it is not a matter of IF we are going to fight, but it's a matter of HOW we fight. We are going to fight, but how we fight is the question. How we fight determines how successful or unsuccessful our relationships are going to be. If you cut yourself off and remain in a cycle of disaffection, you will not be successful in your relationships. You won't be successful in your marriage. You won't be successful in your parent-child relationships because your kids will do things that burn your toast and make you so mad that you don't ever want to talk to them again. You won't be successful your relationships with your mom, dad, sister, brother, aunt, uncle, cousin or anybody else. Any time we are in relationship, we are going to fight, but we have to know how to fight. We're not trying to get weapons so that we can get one up on each other. We are going to get our arsenal together so that we know that when we do fight, we'll be fighting fair. We want to be able to overcome our struggles so that we can be successful in our relations. There is no reason why we who have the Holy Ghost and love the Lord can't be successful in our relationships.

We are going to talk about the cycle of disaffection. The first part of this cycle is stress. I'm sure that we all have faced stress. How do we handle our stress? Stress consists of our everyday pressures: the car payment, going to work, paying bills, our kids getting on our nerves, burning our dinner, ironing and burning a hole in our clothes, people on our jobs getting on our nerves, etc. Stress. Deadlines. These are things that will sometimes throw us into destructive cycles. We have to be able to get a handle on this stuff. We have to learn how to bring our flesh under subjection. That is part of our problem. If we do not bring our flesh under subjection we will constantly find ourselves being defeated in all of these struggles. We have to get to the point where we overcome this.

After stress, we have satanic assault. This is the same as we saw in Genesis 3 when the enemy comes in and questions Eve about what God really said. Isn't it funny that when God gives you instructions the enemy always comes in to bring questions about what you should and shouldn't do when you already know down in your know what God told you to do? Even if you don't get a word from God, in our conscience we know what we should and should not do. Even when we get in relationships with each other, we don't need the Holy Ghost to tell us when we need to apologize. Do you really need God to speak to you to tell you that you need to repent? Our problem is that we always try to make excuses for the flesh. When these assaults come in, we have to begin to know how to overcome the enemy when he attacks us. He attacks our mind and sometimes he uses people to cause disagreement and misunderstandings. You have to know how to fight.

The next thing is scripts from our past. We have to stop reading the stuff from the past. We read those scripts over and over and over again. We read about our abuse, we read about what our family members did to us, and we find ourselves in cycles. We allow what people say to us to trigger thoughts and memories that take us back to what was once done to us. Because of that, we read the script over and over again and we separate ourselves from one another. For instance, you may have a disagreement with someone and what they say to you may remind you of what someone else said to you. Instead of understanding that this is a separate incident, we start connecting the dots. Without realizing it, this situation reminds me of that situation, and because you were hurt in that situation, you feel like you have to protect yourself better in this situation. We start cutting each other off because of how they act and what they say. Even though we don't say it out loud, our behavior says it for us. It could be something as simple as us normally answering a certain person's calls but ignoring the calls when something is triggered. We start changing how we behave with each other because of an old script.

You cannot make people in your present pay for what happened to you in your past. We have got to be delivered from our past. If we don't allow God to deliver us from our past we will continually stay in destructive cycles. It's back to our fight. It's not about IF we are going to fight, it's about HOW we are going to fight. If we are fighting with old scripts, you will not win because those old scripts do not have any new strategies. You can't win this war the same way that you got defeated the last time. If your strategy didn't work last time, it's not going to work this time either. We have to deal with the scripts from our pasts. We also have to deal with our injuries, hurts and bitterness.

Let's look at sin and selfishness. All of us have the propensity to be selfish.

Romans 7:1-3

" Know ye not, brethren, (for I speak to them that know the law,) how that the law hath dominion over a man as long as he liveth? For the woman which hath an husband is bound by the law to her husband so long as he liveth; but if the husband be dead, she is loosed from the law of her husband. So then if, while her husband liveth, she be married to another man, she shall be called an adulteress: but if her husband be dead, she is free from that law; so that she is no adulteress, though she be married to another man."

I am going to use this as an example. We are like that woman whose husband is dead but we don't understand that the husband is dead. We are walking around here still bound by the same stuff, not understanding that we have been freed. We think we're still stuck to the same stuff. We behave like we are still bound by the same old sin and the same old selfishness. We don't realize that those things have died already. I know that this isn't exegetically correct, but you know what I am saying. I'm not trying to exegete the text; I am using this as an example. Paul is saying that if a woman's married, she is vowed to her husband as long as he is alive, but if he dies, she's free. What I'm to say to you is that God has made us free. He's made us free from all this same nonsense and we keep going back to this nonsense as if it's still a part of our life. We have to understand that we have already been made free. It's a horrible thing to be free and not know that you're free. It's a horrible thing to still be walking around in bondage. It's the enemy keeping us under his control when we have already been made free.

I want to skip down to Romans 7:13-25.

"Was then that which is good made death unto me? God forbid. But sin, that it might appear sin, working death in me by that which is good; that sin by the commandment might become exceeding sinful. For we know that the law is spiritual: but I am carnal, sold under sin. For that which I do I allow not: for what I would, that do I not; but what I hate, that do I."

"If then I do that which I would not, I consent unto the law that it is good. Now then it is no more I that do it, but sin that dwelleth in me. For I know that in me (that is, in my flesh,) dwelleth no good thing: for to will is present with me; but how to perform that which is good I find not. For the good that I would I do not: but the evil which I would not, that I do. Now if I do that I would not, it is no more I that do it, but sin that dwelleth in me. I find then a law, that, when I would do good, evil is present with me. For I delight in the law of God after the inward man: But I see another law in my members, warring against the law of my mind, and bringing me into captivity to the law of sin which is in my members. O wretched man that I am! who shall deliver me from the body of this death? I thank God through Jesus Christ our Lord. So then with the mind I myself serve the law of God; but with the flesh the law of sin."

Isn't this something? This was the Apostle Paul. I love that this great and anointed man who was full of the Holy Ghost who healed the sick and raised the dead said all of this. We walk around talking about how we are saved, sanctified and filled with the Holy Ghost but we forget that there is a law that's working in us that we have to overcome. We have the tendency to walk in sin and to be selfish. Paul is saying first of all that he doesn't even understand why he does why he does. This man has deep revelation. He's been up to the third heaven, but he doesn't understand why he does what he does. He understands the mysteries of God but he doesn't understand why he does what he does. He is telling us that there is a war going on in his members that is constantly fighting. That is the same war going on with you and with the person you are in relationship with. When both of you are warring and nobody is listening to the Holy Ghost, you begin to butt heads and clash. We have this war going on, and the thing that we should do we don't do, and we don't even know why we won't do what's right. We know to do it, but we don't do it. On one hand, here we go back to Genesis 3 when we were talking about satanic assault and reading scripts from the past. Here comes the enemy bringing doubt about whether or not we heard clearly from God. We get stuck in this world's mentality, which puts self-preservation first. Let's look back at Romans 7:14-15 which says, "For we know that the law is spiritual: but I am carnal, sold under sin. For that which I do I allow not: for what I would, that do I not; but what I hate, that do I." In other words, "This flesh has a voice and I have been listening to it and doing what it tells me to do, especially when I get angry." When we get angry, we can't hear the voice of God like we're supposed to because we start listening to our own flesh. Paul said that the Law is spiritual but that he was not. He said that he was bound to sin. I'm sure that we can relate to this. I can relate - the things I hate are the things I find myself doing. We don't want to but we want to. Our flesh feels good after we do certain things but then our spirit man is unsettled because of what we have done. What Paul is saying is that there are times that we opt to do for ourselves instead of doing for others. There are times that we choose ourselves over others. Isn't that something? Paul was filled with the Holy Ghost but he still said that he doesn't know how to carry out the will of God. He didn't know how to make it right. He didn't know how to work it out.

This makes me think of when we were talking about unity and we read the example of Solomon talking to the women about the baby. We talked about how in this instance, the real mother could always be identified because the real mother would sacrifice and not kill the baby. We always know where we are in God based on our level of sacrifice. We must look at whether we are able to do for others vs. doing for ourselves. We must evaluate whether we are able to put others on the forefront and forget about our own feelings, emotions and desires. This is hard. It is especially hard when you feel like you are always the underdog and that you are always having to do everything for everybody else, and you always wonder when someone is going to do something for you. We need help because this war is going on in us. It keeps us bound to sin and selfishness. Because of this, we will let our own feelings ruin our relationships and not fight for the baby. Isn't that horrible? We suggest that the baby be split in half. What? Who wants a dead carcass? After a while, it is going to start smelling. It's not going to take anything from you to sacrifice. It is not going to take anything from you to give up whatever you think is right for you and give it for someone else. I know that it is hard. Our nature is trained to look out for self first. We don't know how to do things that our nature is not accustomed to.

In verse 20, Paul says that when he does what he doesn't want to do, it's not him that is doing it, but it is sin that dwells within him. Are you ready for this reality? We have to deal with the sin that is within us. We have sin in us. We don't think we do because we feel like we dot all of our i's and cross all of our t's. I am a perfectionist so I am describing myself as I talk about this. God says, "Wait a minute. It is the sin in you that you have to deal with." If you don't deal with the sin, the sin will make you say that you can't trust anymore. The sin will make you say that you don't want to be bothered with others anymore.

The sin will start building animosity and resentment. All of this gets started because of anger and conflict. When we get into conflict, all of this stuff starts coming out of us. We ask God where it comes from and why we are so angry. One little thing comes up and you will just explode. Anger will come out like a flood and you will be wondering where it came from. You are in a cycle and you didn't even know it. You were on your way in the cycle and did not realize it because you were probably already facing stress about deadlines, people, money and everything else. Then here come the satanic attacks. The enemy starts attacking you and people start letting the devil use them. Then on top of that, you start reading scripts from the past, walking around free and not remembering that you're free, putting yourself in bondage. After that, all of a sudden, here comes that sin nature that stands up in us... with our sanctified selves. Sin stands up. Not the Holy Ghost. Why don't we start speaking in tongues when we get mad? Why don't we go into prayer? Why don't we rebuke ourselves? Why don't we plead the blood of Jesus against us? We will plead the blood against other people in the checkout line at the store. We will not plead it against our sin nature, though. Remember that even when you are not saying anything, you are saying something with your body language, facial expresssions, and gestures.

The Apostle Paul says in verse 21 that when he wants to do right, evil is always present. You don't even have to worry about looking for an occasion for temptation. It will find you. Bad circumstances will find you. Anything that can go wrong will go wrong (Murphy's Law). Verse 22 says that in Paul's spirit, he is delighting in the Law of God. We are the same way. In our spirit, the Word of God is ringing in our hearts. We have the love of Jesus down in our hearts. We have to get the love of Jesus out of our hearts and into our actions. Paul said that he had it in his inner being but it stopped right there. That's our problem. We have it inside but it isn't working on the outside. What good is it if it's only inside and not working outside? That makes us religious. It is religious when what is on the inside hasn't done anything to change you outside appearance, how you behave, what you do and what you say. If all you have is what is on the inside, then guess what? You have to go back and get some more. What you have inside should affect what is outside. This is where the rubber meets the road. Can I really forgive you, or am I not going to do your laundry now because you got on my nerves? "I'm gonna let your dirty clothes sit here and wait and I will see how long it takes for you to get them washed." I have done it. I have let the whole house go and said that I wasn't doing anything because I was thinking about myself. It doesn't matter what someone else does. It matters what you do. The reality is that we have to be honest with ourselves.

Going back to what Paul said; this is Paul talking. This is not someone who just got saved. This is somebody who has had an experience with Jesus who is being used mightily of God and who write two-thirds of the New Testament. He was a smart man. This is what I'm saying. None of that stuff matters until you can get it out of your heart and in your deeds. How are you fighting at home? When it comes down to it, what are you doing? Are you saying everything that you can say so that you can go off on people? Are you making sure that you tell people off on the sly? You have to be careful because you can say words but you cannot take them back. You can't take back what you say once you say it. You can apologize, but there is a seed that has been planted by the words of your mouth. Because we have the Holy Ghost on the inside, we have to remember that life and death is in the power of our tongue. There are things that are set in motion in the realm of the Spirit when we start talking. Good stuff, bad stuff, ugly stuff. There are things that are set in motion when we start saying things that we should not say. We have to get what's on the inside working outside. Let me give you another example. We are quick to say that someone "always" or "never" does something. Nobody ALWAYS does something. Nobody NEVER does something. Are you understanding? We have to be careful even with words like that. They may do it sometimes, but not always. They may not do it all the time, but not never. When you say things like that, you are not giving the person room for the times that they actually do or don't do whatever it is you are speaking of.

Paul is looking at the fact that there is sin and selfishness in us that must be dealt with. Verse 23 says: "But I see another law in my members, warring against the law of my mind, and bringing me into captivity to the law of sin which is in my members." I need to tie this in with the first couple of verses that we read. Here it is that I'm already free, but that old husband from the past (my past is my old husband) keeps showing up trying to tell me that I'm still married to him. He's dead! I don't know you anymore. I'm not connected to you. Why are you still trying to have me connected to you? Why are you still trying to make me feel like I'm bound to you? I'm not bound to you anymore. I'm already free - but there's something in me that keeps telling me that I'm not free and I keep letting that war that's going on in me take over me. As a result, I succumb to the will of my flesh.

Verses 24-25: "O wretched man that I am! Who shall deliver me from the body of this death? I thank God through Jesus Christ our Lord. So then with the mind I myself serve the Law of God; but with the flesh the law of sin." We have to get delivered from the sin and the selfishness that are in us. Yes, Christ has made us free, but we have to get delivered. Some of us are still stuck in Romans 7 and we should not be stuck there. We aren't getting delivered from our flesh, because we're still stuck and won't allow God to be Lord of our lives. If Jesus were really the Lord of our lives, when it came down to it, we would submit to Him and to His will. We would submit to His Word and we would do the things His Word commands us to do. There is so much that we could talk about right here with this sin and selfishness. We can't get stuck here because we have a whole lesson to get through.

These are things that are a part of the cycle of disaffection. That sin starts taking over. The last thing is speed. We always say that we don't have time for things and that we have to go. We are always on the go. We have to be still sometimes. Pump the brakes. Slow it down. For some of us, if someone tells us to slow down, it's like they cursed at us. We have to learn how to relax. If we don't, all of this speed will set us right back to the beginning of this cycle which leads to

273

stress. It starts all over again. When you get stressed out, you get aggravated. When you get aggravated you get into misunderstandings. I know because I have been in the cycle before. I know that this is something we have to be diligent about working on. We want to come out of that cycle.

I want to talk about what we do when we start distancing ourselves. Sometimes we get angry because the things we hope for don't materialize. We have hope for things and when those things don't show up, we become disappointed. The Bible says in Proverbs 13:12 that "hope deferred makes the heart sick." A lot of times, when that disappointment sets in, we lose our vigor. We lose our zeal. We stop striving to do things. We end up taking a backseat to life. We may not say we're discouraged, but those emotions start taking over. Instead of us walking in victory and speaking the Word of God, we allow our emotions to overtake us. We have sin and all that other foolishness, and then our emotions. Lord help us.

I want to talk about the nature of anger. Our anger has a nature. There is something to our anger that takes on a life of its own. Because anger takes on a life of its own in us, it is what causes us to lose out in our relationships. We have to begin to know our own cycles. You have to know what your "switches" are. Let's deal with the results of negative interactions. When we deal with people and have a negative interaction, that is what starts the nature of anger going. We start walking in anger because people lie on us or mistreat us. Then we start showing the faces of anger. Our adrenaline starts rising, we start panting and huffing and puffing, our faces turn red. We start rolling our eyes and rolling our necks. We start pointing our fingers. This is how we present our anger. We are mad and we want those who are mad at to know that we are mad. We start yelling and screaming. We may not yell and scream out loud but inside we yell and scream. I have a big New York mouth and sometimes I yell with this big New York mouth.

This is how we get delivered. Paul talks about this in Romans 7. We have to know what's in us. We have to know that there is a war raging in us, and we have to take authority over this war. It's not until you take authority and be honest about this war that you will see results. We can't go around acting like we are all good when we are at church and then be about to blow someone's brains out when we leave. We start showing all of these faces of anger such as being stubborn, intimidating, threatening, etc. Shouting is not effective communication. Stubbornness is not going to help your communication. Trying to intimidate each other with threats is not going to help your communication.

Let's talk about this one. We withhold love. "You stay on your side of the bed and I will stay on mine." "You go to the man cave, and I'm going in my room. Don't call me, don't talk to me, don't walk next to me, don't smell me, don't touch me, don't look at me. I might put your eyes out. You go sleep on that couch, I'm gonna sleep on this couch." We do this for however long. We stop talking to each other. Did you know that when you withhold communication it's the same thing as withholding love? When you stop talking to people, that's withholding love. "I'm not calling you anymore. I'm not telling you that I'm not calling you; I'm just not going to do it. I'm not gonna answer your text messages." Silence. That's my favorite. We know how to give people the silent treatment. We do it. That is the polar opposite of yelling and screaming. Inside, you're seething. It's not good to do that. These are negative ways that anger shows its face. In us is a law of sin. In us is a war that is raging and telling us not to do what God has told us to do. You have the love of Jesus but you don't share it. When you withhold love and conversation that is a way of starving someone for affection because you're angry.

I pray that we're not engaging in this, but sometimes when we can't get our point across in words, we result to violence. We start throwing blows. We start throwing things. Breaking stuff. You spent all that money on stuff and then you throw it across the room and break it. This is a part of the Gospel of Jesus Christ too. We have to get our anger under control. One of the fruit of the spirit is self-control (Galatians 5:22-23). That's our problem. We would rather someone else try to control us than to exhibit self-control. God wants you to control you. It's nobody else's fault that you can't control you. It's sin in you that causes you not to be able to control yourself. We want to get away from these negative interactions and these negative behaviors. We want to get away from the negative ways that anger presents itself.

Now I want to hit on a couple of reasons why people get angry. Proverbs 15:1 says, "A soft answer turneth away wrath: but grievous words stir up anger." The English Standard Version of that verse says, "A soft answer turns away wrath, but a harsh word stirs up anger." You get angry and say something to me, and then I get angry because of how you said what you said. We say nasty things to each other and that is why we end up angry. How are we fighting? We're fighting with nasty words. We're saying mean things to each other. We're saying stuff that we know is going to provoke us to anger. We know those words will get a reaction out of the other person. That's why we say it. We put people down with our words. When we start fighting, we say all kinds of things. The one thing that stands in our way all the time is our pride. Harsh words are what make us angry.

Proverbs 16:28 (ESV): "A dishonest man spreads strife, and a whisperer separates close friends."

One of the things that make us angry is betrayal and gossip. Gossip and lies make us angry. Jesus said that we would face this in the last days. What's wrong with us if we can't take it? I'm not telling you that you won't feel it, but you have to be able to process it and let it go. You can't let it make you into a different person. God is holding you accountable for how you respond. God is not holding me accountable for how someone else responds to me. He is holding me accountable for how I respond. I am responsible for my own reactions and responses. If I have not responded right, I need to get it right.

Proverbs 17:14 (ESV): "The beginning of strife is like letting out water, so quit before the quarrel breaks out."

Do we know to do that? Do we know how to stop things before they happen? You can see that you are headed for a head=on collision. Instead of pumping the breaks, we step on the gas. Instead of slowing things down, we speed things up. We retaliate. Here comes that war. Quarrels and frustration are another reason why we are angry. We are angry because we are arguing. We don't like how people did the things they did. It is like water bursting out of a dam. It's like someone put a hole in the wall of the dam and all of the water comes rushing out. We just let it all hang out. We hold on to stuff for a long time and then we get to the point that we can't hold it in any longer and we let it out and tell people off with no concern of whether they like it or not. We act like we are sanctified and we don't have thoughts like that, but we do. We have to work this out.

This is why Paul said in verse 24, "Oh wretched man that I am!" In other words, "I have so much stuff that I need you to work on in me." We are so glad that we can go to Jesus. We are so glad that He gives us grace so that we can make it through this stuff. Let's look to Jesus, but let's not destroy our relationships because of the war that is going on within. Don't get your relationships go. You will regret it in the end. Don't let your relationships go with your family or with your spouses. It seems like in the church, we will forgive strangers before

279

we forgive each other. Somebody on the outside can do something to us and we will forgive them, but let someone in our house do us wrong. We go back to those faces of anger: shouting, silence and withholding love. We go back to all those things. We have to get delivered.

Proverbs 22:24 (ESV): "Make no friendship with a man given to anger, nor go with a wrathful man"

A lot of times, the anger that we feel is by our association. I don't have anything to be mad at, but because Sally was mad, I got mad because Sally was mad. Don't be following, hanging out or making friends with an angry man. We are in a cycle and we don't know it. We have a war in our flesh and we put it all over social media. We don't even have to call or text to gossip now. All we have to do is get on Facebook. People have nothing to be mad at but they make friends with someone who is given to anger. Because we associate with them, we get mad because they are mad. It's in the Word. Not just that, it could be a generational thing. Your grandmother could be angry, and then your parents were angry, and now you are angry. I am the oldest of my father's children, and every last one of us has had to overcome that stronghold of anger. My dad used to ride around with a gun in his car threatening people and saying that he would blow their brains out. I would have to talk to my brothers and tell them that they could not let that anger overcome them. I would tell them that they needed to pray and ask God to help them so that the anger wouldn't rule them. I understand the generational curse and the gene pool from the angry man, but you can be delivered from that. First, you have to want it and you have to realize it. We all have different temperaments but me have to make sure that we are not hooking up with people who have angry temperaments who are not trying to walk in self-control.

Proverbs 14:29 (ESV): "Whoever is slow to anger has great understanding, but he who has a hasty temper exalts folly."

How is it that we are so quick to get angry? We get angry before we even hear the whole story. That means that we are running and exalting foolishness. That's what folly is. When we are hasty, we will make mistakes. We could be wrong because we didn't hear the whole matter. We have to be honest about the war that is going on. The war looks different in each of us but it is still going on. You cannot be hasty. You want to make sure that you don't make these mistakes. You will walk away from relationships and regret it later if you move in haste. You have to learn how to cool down. Have a cooling off period. Think first. Look before you leap. Don't make hasty choices. Take your time and hear God. If God isn't speaking to you by His Spirit, then pick up the Bible and He will speak to you through His Word.

I want to switch gears and look at Ephesians 4:26 in the ESV: "Be angry and do not sin; do not let the sun go down on your anger" This is something we need to practice. We need to be able deal with our anger without sinning. There is a way to be angry and not sin. We know how to be angry but we don't know how to refrain from sin. I want to go over three things that will help us accomplish this.

1: You have to have a safe place with each other. You have to have a place where you can come and express yourselves and disagree without being threatened or abandoned.

2: Manage your anger. James 1:19-20 talks about our anger. Psalm 38:7 talks about managing our anger. We just read Proverbs 14:39 about not being hasty. That is managing your anger. You must manage your emotions. You have to learn how to respond and not react. A reaction is playing tit for tat. A response is taking a moment to think about the situation before saying or doing anything. Delay is the greatest response you can ever have when you're angry. This is not a television show. You are not required to beat a buzzer and give quick answers. You don't need any of that. Haste causes mistakes. Get outside help if it's necessary. That's how you manage. Can we have a sidebar? When you get the help, it is imperative that you follow the instructions that the help is giving you. Otherwise, you are wasting your time.

3: Let love rule. Remember 1 Corinthians 13. We need to print this Scripture and hang it around our house. We need to memorize it. We have to exercise forgiveness and patience. We have to understand that our covenant to each other is that we are going to be loyal to each other at any cost. I don't care what it costs. I don't care if people call us crazy. We are going to be loyal at any cost because of love.

Let's look at 1 Corinthians 13. This has to be our goal. You have to work at this together. You and your spouse have to work on this together. You and those who you are in relationship with have to be committed to these principles. You have to be committed to do whatever it takes to see this thing through.

1 Corinthians 13:1-13

If I speak in the tongues of men and of angels, but have not love, I am a noisy gong or a clanging cymbal. And if I have prophetic powers, and understand all mysteries and all knowledge, and if I have all faith, so as to remove mountains, but have not love, I am nothing. If

I give away all I have, and if I deliver up my body to be burned, but have not love, I gain nothing.

Love is patient and kind; love does not envy or boast; it is not arrogant or rude. It does not insist on its own way; it is not irritable or resentful it does not rejoice at wrongdoing, but rejoices with the truth. Love bears all things, believes all things, hopes all things, endures all things.Love never ends. As for prophecies, they will pass away; as for tongues, they will cease; as for knowledge, it will pass away. For we know in part and we prophesy in part, but when the perfect comes, the partial will pass away. When I was a child, I spoke like a child, I thought like a child, I reasoned like a child. When I became a man, I gave up childish ways. For now we see in a mirror dimly, but then face to face. Now I know in part; then I shall know fully, even as I have been fully known. So now faith, hope, and love abide, these three; but the greatest of these is love.

Love is not an emotion. Love is an action word. Love has to become a verb and not a noun. It's not just a person, place or thing. It is what you do even when you don't want to do it. We don't want to split the baby in half. We want the baby to be alive. Find a way to make it work. When I love you I'm going to find a way to work it work. Why? Because we are going to be loyal to each other at any cost.

I could put my life on the line and die for this gospel, but if I don't have love, it means nothing. If love is not at the root of everything I'm doing, I have wasted my time.

Can we deal with our secret jealousies? Sometimes this is the root of why we are fighting: 'There is something in me that doesn't appreciate whatever it is that you have going on.' That happens in relationships. We have to deal with this stuff. I shouldn't be jealous of you talking to your friends, and you shouldn't be jealous of me talking to mine. We are going to be loyal to each other until the end, so nobody could ever take your place. I have to let that sink all the way in.

There is no pride in love. I'm not going to try to boast myself ahead of you because I am looking out for you first and not myself. Somebody has to be the one who is willing to humble themselves down. Somebody has to be willing to risk their reputation. Somebody has to be willing to love in spite of what anyone else thinks, does or says. This has to be our mentality. The reason why we can't do that for each other is because we really don't love. We love with limits and conditions. We love people as long as they do what we want them to do. We have to get our love right. What is going on with you is nobody else's fault. You have to deal with yourself and your love walk. Love puts others first. This is the Gospel of Jesus Christ. If we could get this right in our marriages and all of our relationships, we would be much better. Considering how what I say is going to affect you should be more important than me having my say. I'm not saying not to say things that need to be said. However, rudeness and arrogance are not love. Are you saying what you want to say because you want to say it, or are you promoting love?

Remember that love bears all things. This means that you are going to carry whatever you have to carry for as long as you have to carry it because you love. We don't have it like we thought we did. Love believes all things. Another translation says that love believes the good. I'm not trying to point out your weaknesses and see where you are going to fall. Love is looking for the good in the other individual. Can we do that instead of pointing out each other's faults? We can see each other's faults from miles away, but can we believe the good in each other? You have to make yourself believe the good, especially when the bad has presented itself. We have to ask God to change our perspective and to help us to see the good in things and in people. If

286

we were really reading this Word and seeing what God was saying, we would look like Jesus. Because we're not investing the time in studying and applying His Word, we don't look like what we should. We sing the song "I Don't Look Like What I've Been Through" but we don't look like Jesus either. We have to get that right. Love believes all things, bears all things and hopes all things. We have to stand with each other and believe God with each other until the end. We have to believe God for people even when they can't believe God for themselves. We have to trust God even when others give up their faith. Why? Because we love them. That is real love. We have to get it like that. Relationships are hard and challenging. Relationships will pull things out of you that you didn't even know was in you. Relationships will make you respond in unfavorable ways.

We have to go back and we have to get this right. It takes humility. Love is not arrogant. If you're holding on to the wrongs and to your position that you are right, you are not walking in love. If you're trying to have your own way, you're not walking in love. Love is not going to insist on its own way. Love is going to find a way to show that it is love. Love is going to let your brother or your sister have the right of way. Love is going to make sure that your brother or your sister or your spouse understands that they are first. That's what love is going to do. It's hard because we have stuff in us. We are fighting to be first when we need to put others first. God forbid if you grow up being the underdog - you were always the last to get everything. You were always the last person everybody thought about, you were always picked on, everybody always left you out and you were never the first choice. If that's the case, then this is going to be more difficult for you to set somebody else out in front of you. You feel like you deserve to be first. No, we want this love walk right. Love endures all things. That means that love never gives up. I'm not going to give up on you because I love you. I'm not going to give up on what I believe for you because I love you.

If you walk way, it's because your love is not where it should be. As Paul said, the Law is spiritual but we are not. We think we're spiritual but we're not. The reason I know that we're not spiritual is because we can't endure with each other. We give up on each other. We kick each other to the curb. I want us to take the time to work on our love. Work on being angry and sinning not. Keep working on it until you get it. You've got a whole lot of time ahead of you to get this right. Keep working on it until you get it.

Chapter 13

Keep It Moving

Philippians 3:7-16 (ESV)

7But whatever gain I had, I counted as loss for the sake of Christ. Indeed, I count everything as loss because of the surpassing worth of knowing Christ Jesus my Lord. For his sake I have suffered the loss of all things and count them as rubbish, in order that I may gain Christ and be found in him, not having a righteousness of my own that comes from the law, but that which comes through faith in Christ, the righteousness from God that depends on faith— 10 that I may know him and the power of his resurrection, and may share his sufferings, becoming like him in his death, that by any means possible I may attain the resurrection from the dead. Not that I have already obtained this or am already perfect, but I press on to make it my own, because Christ Jesus has made me his own. Brothers, I do not consider that I have made it my own. But one thing I do: forgetting what lies behind and straining forward to what lies ahead, I press on toward the goal for the prize of the upward call of God in Christ Jesus. Let those of us who are mature think this way, and if in anything you think otherwise, God will reveal that also to you. 16 Only let us hold true to what we have attained.

I would like to bring your attention to the Message Bible's translation of this passage because I like the way the Message Bible tells us off. I like the way it puts us in our place and corrects us so nicely that while we think we're reading something encouraging, we're really getting told off.

"The very credentials these people are waving around as something special, I'm tearing up and throwing out with the trash—along with everything else I used to take credit for. And why? Because of Christ. Yes, all the things I once thought were so important are gone from my life. Compared to the high privilege of knowing Christ Jesus as my Master, firsthand, everything I once thought I had going for me is insignificant—dog dung. I've dumped it all in the trash so that I could embrace Christ and be embraced by him. I didn't want some petty, inferior brand of righteousness that comes from keeping a list of rules when I could get the robust kind that comes from trusting Christ—God's righteousness.

I gave up all that inferior stuff so I could know Christ personally, experience his resurrection power, be a partner in his suffering, and go all the way with him to death itself. If there was any way to get in on the resurrection from the dead, I wanted to do it.

Focused on the Goal I'm not saying that I have this all together, that I have it made. But I am well on my way, reaching out for Christ, who has so wondrously reached out for me. Friends, don't get me wrong: By no means do I count myself an expert in all of this, but I've got my eye on the goal, where God is beckoning us onward—to Jesus. I'm off and running, and I'm not turning back. So let's keep focused on that goal, those of us who want everything God has for us. If any of you have something else in mind, something less than total commitment, God will clear your blurred vision—you'll see it yet! Now that we're on the right track, let's stay on it."

290

As I was reading this and in prayer seeking the Lord, something dropped in my spirit. One of the things we have to learn how to do is praise God for "already" even though we're living in our "not yet". We know that there are things we are believing for and things that God has promised to us, but we are still living in our "not yet". Do you have everything that God promised you? There are still some things that we're waiting on for God to do in us and through us, and so we have to learn how to give God glory and praise while we're waiting on Him and living in our "not yet".

Let's look at a couple of verses here. Paul in verse seven says that he had something that he ought to have status because of, but he said that he was getting rid of it. Paul found out that having a good education, good credentials, and the praise of man is not enough. It's not enough. Having a good name among everybody else is not enough. God is calling for us to do more. What is it that He needs us to do? He needs us to keep it moving.

I've found out that there are people who like to look at you and keep you in your past and what happened last night, last week, last

291

month, and last year. One of the things you have to learn how to do is that even though you understand that your credentials mean nothing, you have to understand that your past means absolutely nothing. That means that you can't hold anything over anybody else's head. Aren't we good for doing stuff like that? Aren't we good for telling folks "I remember when..."?'" Aren't we good for reminding people how many times they have gotten saved and backslidden? Paul said that he was getting rid of all of the stuff that everybody else counts as weighty. He got rid of all the stuff that everybody else thought made him something. He was finding out that all of it was worthless. It means nothing in the face of God, and God isn't even interested in it. He's not impressed with it. He doesn't care anything about it. We are the ones that get caught up in that nonsense. Don't we?

I watch sometimes how people have these ordinations and they dress up like the Pope. We think that makes us something because we paid $5,000 for a ring. We were somewhere and someone was talking about how their previous overseer had spent $15,000 to be made an apostle. The devil is a liar. This is the stuff that man has begun to say, "This is what makes you what you are." Nobody wants to come to the little white church on the little corner because they don't think there's much of anything in there. Nobody wants to come to the rundown spot because they don't think there's anything in there. I've learned something from my husband; he likes to eat at the rundown spots. He says that's where the best food is. Myself on the other hand, I'm picky. I'm the one who doesn't want to go in there.

The thing about it is that this world is caught up in appearances. This world is caught up in status, and God does not care about our status. What He really wants to know is if you love Him. Are you obedient? Are you following His instructions? Are you walking in humility towards Him? This is what God is concerned about. He's not concerned about how many dollars we put in the offering. He wants us to give, but He's not concerned about that as much as He's concerned with our lifestyle. It's about our lifestyle.

I love that Paul told on himself. It's funny because we like to tell on everybody else but we don't like to tell on ourselves. When are you gonna have a "tell on you" day? When will you point the fingers at yourself so that you don't make others feel inferior? That goes especially for leaders. The Body of Christ is in a messed up state. We are so confused. We're thinking that God wants us to be superstars.

293

Did you ever see that on Saturday Night Live? That's what we want. We want our names in lights. There is a song Jason Upton sings about a dying star. If you really want to be a star for Jesus, you're going to have to die. We don't want to die. We want to live so bad that we would do anything to live. We would pay top dollar if we thought it would give us a couple of extra years. Paul was saying that if there was any way that he could be included in the resurrection of the dead, he was going to do it. Is that your mentality? Do you want to do whatever it takes so that when you leave this earth you can see Jesus again? Our goal should not be trying to get a nice house and a nice car. I like that stuff, and I appreciate the Lord for my five acres. But guess what? When I leave here, those five acres are going to be right here. I'm not taking any of that with me: none of those rocks, none of those potholes, none of it. All of that stuff is going to be right here. Our problem is that we don't put weight on the things that matter. We don't put value on the things God has declared to be weighty. Paul is trying to bring everybody into the realization that priorities are important. Even in our time of worship, it's hard for us to break through because we are worried about what we are going through, how the music sounds, and how long we are going to be in church. When you are truly in worship, you are not concerned about time or about what is going on around you. All you want to do is get a hold of God and everything else around you becomes worthless. When are we going to get to the point where we realize that everything else is worthless?

Paul said that being religious is not enough. Going to church is not enough. Being smart or sounding smart is not enough. Looking good is not enough. Being able to hold a conversation with good people who know how to have good conversation is not enough. Having money is not enough. There is something that God has done. He has arrested me for this purpose. I don't understand this purpose, and because I don't understand everything that he has arrested me for, I have to spend the rest of my life trying to figure out why I have been arrested. I have to figure out why God has laid hold of my heart. I have to figure out why God has laid His hands on me. I have to figure out why God has pulled me out of sin and into Him. What is it that He wants from my life? That's the question.

Paul was talking about all of the frailties of life. I can wear my skirt down to the floor, I can take my earrings out, I can take off my makeup, I can walk around here looking like a mammy, but that is not going to save me. I tried it. Have you ever tried it? I looked saved but

I was not saved. You couldn't tell that I was out fornicating because my skirt was long. We try to make things look good. We want things to look easy. This is hard. Paul was talking about being arrested. When you are arrested, you have no will. I want you to try to go to the jail and tell those prisoners to do what they want. They have to go to bed when someone tells them to go to bed. They have to wash their hind parts when someone gives them the opportunity to do so. When they get a lockdown, that's where they have to be until somebody comes with the keys. You have to understand that this is what has happened to you when you gave your life to Christ. You have no say-so. You have absolutely no say-so. You belong to Him, and whatever He says is what you have to do.

We have to learn that God is not playing with us. We want to shout, we want to speak in tongues, we want to look good, and we want our name in lights. But are you going to die? Are you ready to die? Are you ready to read your eulogy in front of everybody else and say "Here lays me, and I'm done." Are we ready to do that? We have to keep it moving. Paul already knew that he had stuff going on with him every day, but he also knew that God had arrested him. He had to find out why God had arrested him, and he was determined that he was not going to stop until he got the answer.

Let's look at the King James translation of verse twelve: "Not as though I had already attained, either were already perfect: but I follow after, if that I may apprehend that for which also I am apprehended of Christ Jesus." There are so many people who preach and try to act like they are perfect. Paul had something different to say. We don't have it all together. I wasn't at the club last night, but I still don't have it all together. I wasn't out smoking and drinking but I still don't have it together. Paul said, "Don't look at me and think I have it all together. I'm still praising God for 'already' even though I'm living in my 'not yet'." He didn't get it yet, but he was going to press into God until he got what God said he needed to have. There wasn't even a guarantee that Paul would be able to touch God like God had touched him, but he was determined to find out. I don't want to be an apostle so I can travel and have people give me money. I don't want to be a prophet so that God can give me whatever I want. I want to do what God wants me to do because I want Him to get the glory out of my life so that I might be able to touch Him back like He touched me. This is the Gospel of Jesus Christ. Not "claim your car" or "claim your spouse". I wish someone would just name and claim Jesus already. Why can't anybody do that? They aren't saying that because that comes with a price. Paul let them know that he had not arrived yet. Those people didn't know the tears Paul cried. They didn't know the hell he went through. They didn't know the issues Paul faced. He was saying that he didn't want them looking at him like he was just so wonderful.

We've got it twisted. The best seat in the house is the seat on the pew. What angers me is when people don't want to do anything for God. How does your Holy Ghost let you sit at home and not go to church? How does your Holy Ghost not convict you about not getting up and serving God? How does your Holy Ghost let you do that? Have you received the Holy Ghost since you believed? That's the question we need to ask. The real Holy Ghost convicts of sin. I don't understand that kind of salvation. God has arrested me, and because I'm in His custody, I can't do what I want to do. I can't say what I want to say. Even when I do say what I want to say and do what I want to do, I get convicted and I have to go back and repent. Do we like doing that? That would be a no and a no.

We have been arrested. Think about that. "You have the right to remain silent. Anything you say can and will be used against you in the presence of the Lord. You do not have a right to an attorney. Why? Because your attorney can't get you out of this one." Jesus is going to have to be your attorney. He's the defending attorney, He's the prosecuting attorney, AND He's the judge. You can't win. You'd better believe that He is going to get what He wants regardless. You may as well set your heart to be obedient. Do you know what they do to prisoners who don't want to submit? They lock them in solitary confinement. They get thrown in the hole because they don't know how to listen. They lock them up until they get submitted. God knows how to make everything shut down. He knows how to make it so that you don't get that money you've been waiting on. He knows what to allow so that you will learn to submit.

Verses thirteen and fourteen in the King James translation states: "Brethren, I count not myself to have apprehended: but this one thing I do, forgetting those things which are behind, and reaching forth unto those things which are before, I press toward the mark for the prize of the high calling of God in Christ Jesus." Paul said that he had one focus. Even if he didn't get there today, he knew that he would wake up tomorrow and keep reaching. It doesn't matter what kind of circumstances and failures we are going through we have to keep reaching. Do you know what I'm thankful for? I'm thankful for every time I fell and somebody saw me. Do you know why? Because people laugh when you fall. Some people will even try to record a video of people falling, especially if they fall bad or tear up stuff on their way down. But you need to thank God for every time someone saw an imperfection. You need to thank God for every time you have looked torn up from the floor up. Why? Because you were showing somebody how we do this. This is how you walk in humility. Paul looked like he had it but he knew he didn't have it. You don't hear a lot of people saying that. We are so full of ourselves, but like the song says, we are dying stars. There was a sister in New Jersey who used to sing a song: "I am a star, that's what I are." She was a star in her own mind. You have people today who think they are stars. YouTube has made us our own stars. Socialcam has made us our own stars. As if we need something else to see a couple more hours of you.

Paul knew that he was handcuffed even though it looked like his hands were free. When businessmen get arrested, a lot of times they put their hands together and throw a jacket over them. They hide their handcuffs, but believe me: they are wearing them. Paul had cuffs on him.

If I am going to be able to walk this out, there are some things I am going to have to have selective amnesia about. I choose to forget.

When everybody else wants to remember, I'm choosing to forget. Everybody chooses to remember when you fell and cut your tail in front of everybody, but I choose to forget. All of my family chooses to remember Fran. I'm forgetting about Fran because we need to put her in a box and put her under the ground. How many of us hate our flesh that much? I can't stand this nasty flesh. Paul had to forget about what he feared. He had to forget about how he had failed. He forgot about what he didn't do, what he should have done, and what he could have done. He forgot about all of that stuff because he had to keep it moving. God knows; if you don't let go of what you think and what you think people think, you will never get anywhere. Progress is all about your own perception. Is the glass half full or is it half empty? How you see a thing matters. It doesn't matter how someone else might see it unless I believe what they see. It matters how you see what pertains to you. You're not going to be able to keep it moving if you're stuck in yesterday. The enemy would love nothing more than to keep you stuck in yesterday. As a matter of fact, he wants to keep you stuck in an hour ago. He wants to keep you stuck in five minutes ago. You have to keep moving until you see what God has promised you come to pass.

One of the things I want to look at is the definition of the word "press" used in verse fourteen. That word is from the Greek word "dioko" and it describes a pursuit. It's following something. It also means to flee one thing to follow something else. It means running from one thing to run to another thing. So in essence, what he's saying is that he had to be able to press into God, but in order for him to do that, he had to flee anything that would jeopardize him getting close to God. If I'm going to press in, I have to press against. I have to press against what's trying to keep me from getting to where God called me to. You have to press against everything that jeopardizes your relationship with Him. I don't care if it's people. This word "press" also means to persecute. Sometimes you just have to cut stuff off. Your enemies don't love you. I don't know why you try to be friends with your enemies - they don't love you. Keep it moving. We have to go the distance. Our problem is that we gain ground and then we lose momentum. And then we gain ground and then we lose momentum. And then, we gain ground. And then we lose our momentum. You cannot lose your momentum. Paul is talking about running a race. Even though you may get tired, even though you are gasping for air, and even though you feel like you can't breathe and that the place you're in is closing up on you, you have to keep moving. You have to realize that you are not at the finish line yet. In order for you to get to the finish line, you have to press against and press into. You have to press against what jeopardizes your relationship and press into God. That takes effort.

Here is where your worth ethic is going to have to kick in. Some of us are a little lazy. We have our moments where we don't want to get out of the bed. Think about those days when it's raining and cold. All I want is some hot cocoa and my covers. We have stuff to do and we cannot afford to lose our momentum. Do you know what happens when you are running in a race and you stop and others are running behind you? You become trampled. You get trampled on the ground and everyone else runs over you and stepping on you. You have to keep it in your mind that you've got to keep it moving. Even if I'm doing it with tears in my eyes, I've got to keep moving. Even if I feel like I'm doing it by myself, I have to keep moving. Even if I don't understand why I have to do it a certain way, I have to keep moving. Even though I'm praising God for "already" while I'm living in my "not yet", I have to keep it moving. It doesn't matter what anybody else is saying. It doesn't matter who's whispering or who's pointing fingers. It doesn't matter who has something smart to say. People will always have something smart to say. This is your self-help moment. Lay hands on yourself and say, "Self, somebody is always going to have something to say about what I do. So I might as well keep it moving." You might as well. Even when you've given your all, there will be someone to come along and tell you what you should have done. Do you remember how they used to tell you in school that when you point your finger at somebody, you have three fingers pointing back at you? We forget about that. We like to put the blame on everybody else but ourselves. Today is our hour in which we have to look at where we are, what we feel like we have, what we feel like we have accomplished, and who it is that we feel like we are. We really have to get serious about this.

Let's go to Hebrews 12:1-3 in the Message Bible:

Do you see what this means—all these pioneers who blazed the way, all these veterans cheering us on? It means we'd better get on with it. Strip down, start running—and never quit! No extra spiritual fat, no parasitic sins. Keep your eyes on Jesus, who both began and finished this race we're in. Study how he did it. Because he never lost sight of where he was headed—that exhilarating finish in and with God—he could put up with anything along the way: Cross, shame, whatever. And now he's there, in the place of honor, right alongside God. When you find yourselves flagging in your faith, go over that story again, item by item, that long litany of hostility he plowed through. That will shoot adrenaline into your souls!

Stop wasting time! Stop waiting for somebody else to come along and validate you. You have to know who you are and that Jesus is on the inside of you. You have to know that because Jesus is on the inside of you, you have what you need to do what He called you to do. Strip down, start running, and never quit. I'm going to remind you all of the background on this. We talked before about how there is a generation that we will never see. There is also a generation that has gone on before us. This is the generation that Paul is talking about. They are peering down out of heaven watching you and expecting you to get the job done. They couldn't get the promise without us and we couldn't get the promise without them. There is a people coming after us; that if we're not positive about what we do for God, we're not going to leave any legacy for them when we leave here. This is not just about you, your four, and no more. This is about what God has called you to leave in the earth. So here the writer is saying that you need to pay

305

attention to all of these pioneers who blazed the way and all of these veterans who are cheering us on. Strip down, start running, and never quit. Shed the excess spiritual fat. Get rid of the parasitic sin. Keep your eyes on Jesus. Why? Because He finished the race. He already won, which means that we win. You have to understand that you win. If you are walking around with a defeated mindset and taking on the world's culture, you won't be able to live this life. We have to wear this world loosely. It's nice while we're here, but we have to wear it loosely. The nicest things in life are nothing in comparison to fulfilling our course. You cannot afford any spiritual fat. You can't afford to have anything standing in your way. Stop making excuses for you. What are you gonna say when you stand before God? What could you possibly tell Him? You can't ask Him for a little more time. You can't stand before Him talking about how people get on your nerves.

Jesus never lost sight of where He was headed. That's our problem. We lose sight of where we're going. This is not just about God blessing us. There is a literal place we are trying to get to, and that's a place of maturity in Him. If we are going to keep making excuses for ourselves, we will never get to that place. I like going to the movies sometimes, but how can I go and pray after I just got finished watching him and her and they and they do what they're doing? A PG-rated movie is the old R-rated movie. Even in a PG movie, they have homosexuals sliding up in there. Everybody is kissing each other in the mouth. How can we then come and try to lay hands? Keep your hands to yourself. I want to know what you watched last night first. I want to start interviewing folks before they come in here talking about wanting to lay hands. I need to know what your daily diet is before you try to lay hands. I don't want any of that filthiness in my spirit. Then I go home and I'm fighting with all of this stuff because of someone laying hands. I didn't have that before. What is that? Because we don't interview folks. Keep your dirty hands to yourself.

Somebody got mad because one of the preachers said something about people being a pastor who can't be in the same room with children? I have an answer for that: it's called "disqualified". I understand that Jesus forgives, but if you cannot be left in the room with children because you have been labeled a pedophile, I'm sorry, but no microphone and no sacred desk for you. I have a pew that will fit you nicely. We have no qualifications for people. We're not holding on to the standard of the Word of God. We let anything go.

Everything doesn't go. This is what Paul was talking about. What are the patriarchs seeing when they peer down and look at what we're doing? What are you doing? If we couldn't do this, God would have never called us. By His grace, according to Philippians 4:13, we can do all things through Christ who strengthens us. You have to get yourself in Christ for this to apply. We can't do it in ourselves. We have to lose this picture that we have of stardom. Jesus is the only star. Nobody else's name needs to be in lights but His. Now you may go to the church down the street or around the corner and see that they have their blinking signs on. Blinking lights are a sign of desperation, and we aren't desperate like that. We're desperate for Him, but we are not desperate to draw any and everything. Everybody doesn't want God. Paul said for us to lay aside the weight and the sin that so easily besets us (Hebrews 12:1). It is easy for things to set us back. This is the age of marriages being destroyed, kids going crazy, church folks going crazy... The program they put on TV about first ladies is outrageous. Are you kidding me? These people are not qualified to stand behind the desk. We should be outraged. Where are the prophets that are going to prophesy "Sit down because you aren't of God"? That's the kind of boldness we need. If you're not going to be bold like that, don't you say you're a prophet. That's real ministry. That's real anointing.

That's real mantle. You have to be able to lay aside the weight and the sin so that you can stand up and preach the Word with power. It is hard, but there is a work that God has called us to do. Believe me that the time is coming in which all this fluff and all this pretty stuff will wear out. People are seeing that this stuff is not working. You have to have something to stand on in God. You have to be able to know that it takes time in prayer and fasting. It takes time in the Word. Even though I wish we had a magic wand that we could wave and just get it, that is not our reality. We have to get in the press just like Paul said. This is a press because while I'm trying to get a hold of God, there are things that are pressing against me. There are circumstances that are pressing against you. The thoughts and opinions of others are pressing against you. How other people feel is pressing against you. You have to be able to press against that so that you can get in God.

How many times have you started on your way to do something and you thought about what someone thought about it, and it completely threw you off? That has happened. I don't care what our title is - that has happened. We care what people think. We have to get to the place that we start caring about what God thinks. If we don't care about what God thinks, that's where our problems lie. We have to care about what God's mind is for us. This is the will of God for us. I don't want church to just be a social gathering. This can't be about socializing. I don't care about filling up every pew. Yes I want us to reach people, but I want us to reach people who want God. I want us to do what God has set for us to do. I don't want us to do what everybody else is doing down the road. There is a work that God has put in each of our hands, and we have to be faithful to that call. It's not going to come easy. You will have to lay aside some things, some folks, and your own thoughts so that you can walk in fullness and accomplish the will of God.

You are going to have to read these Scriptures over and over again. Living for the Lord is not a cakewalk. We have good days and bad days. When you start talking about living separated from this world, you will be called a fanatic. It's okay to go to a football game and yell and scream and act a fool, but I have to come to church and be quiet? That ain't happening. I like to yell. You have to go over these Scriptures and see what Jesus did. He endured the cross because He knew what was waiting on the other side. You have to keep your focus on the promise God has made for us. John 14 talks about how Jesus has gone to prepare a place for us so that where He is, there we may be also. I want to get to that place because this world right here has enough turmoil. We have to learn how to keep it moving. We have to learn how to go the distance. I don't care about how many tears we have to cry. I don't care if we're feeling like we're lonely and we just can't make it. We can do all things through Christ who strengthens us. We have to keep it moving. You have no choice - you have been apprehended by God. Now it is up to you to find out why God has arrested you. What does He want out of your life? What is it that He is looking for from you? I can't answer that for you but you have to answer that question. Why are you here? What does He want from you? Why are you saved today? There is a call of God on every last one of us. You can't let your anger, your attitude, how you feel or what you think get in the way of that. I pray that no matter what difficulty we face, we will keep it moving and not be moved.

.

Other Books/CD'S By this Author

The Battle of the Overcomer: A Spiritual Warfare Guide
for the Believer

ISBN-13: 978-1469904160 (CreateSpace-Assigned)
ISBN-10: 1469904160
BISAC: Religion / Christian Life / Spiritual Warfare

The School of Prophetic Mobilization Manual

ISBN-13: 978-1477412138 (CreateSpace-Assigned)
ISBN-10: 1477412131
BISAC: Religion / Christian Ministry / General

Audio CD'S

Every Chapter covered inside Girl, Get A Grip! Is available as an audio message as presented before a LIVE audience/worship service. Audios may be ordered by chapter title

Additional CD titles are available on our website

Sure Word Ministries is an Apostolic/Prophetic, Non-denominational ministry that is striving to bring healing for the "whole man" through the preaching of the Gospel of Jesus Christ, providing transitional housing, conferences, establishing leaders and ministries in the faith, as well as providing instruction through various training programs geared to enhance one's knowledge of God's Word and His love for His creation.

Speaking Ministry

Francesca Stubbs is an Apostle of Jesus Christ who is a seasoned speaker for many different situations that arise: Men/Women's groups/conferences, Seminars, Revivals, etc.

Sure Word Ministries
P.O. Box 229
Spring Lake, NC 28390
(910) 239-7923
(910) 321-5964
www.swdac.org
sureword@swdac.org

For More Resources-Visit us online at: www.swdac.org
To Order –Visit our website or call: (910) 239-7923

Connect with us on Social Media

Facebook.com/apostlefran2014

Twitter.com/ApostleFran